IN THE KINGDOM OF THE FAIRIES

IN THE KINGDOM
OF THE FAIRIES

Susan Coyne

A MEMOIR OF A MAGICAL SUMMER
AND A REMARKABLE FRIENDSHIP

ST. MARTIN'S PRESS
NEW YORK

www.stmartins.com

Library of Congress Cataloging-in-Publication Data

Coyne, Susan.
    In the kingdom of the fairies : a memoir of a magical summer and a remarkable friendship / Susan Coyne.—1st. U.S. ed.
        p. cm.
    ISBN 0-312-31706-9
    1. Coyne, Susan—Childhood and youth. 2. Actors—Canada—Biography. I. Title.

PN2308.C59A3 2003
792'.028'092—dc21
[B]   2003043136

Illustration: Cliff Alejandro
Text Design: Carol Moskot

First published in Canada under the title Kingfisher Days by Random House Canada

First U.S. Edition: August 2003

10 9 8 7 6 5 4 3 2 1

It is requir'd you do awake your faith . . .

The Winter's Tale

for parties she is called ...
When the cats saw my ...
know that I was not on ...

To see a World in a Grain of Sand
And a Heaven in a Wild Flower,
Hold Infinity in the palm of your hand
And Eternity in an hour.

When I first read those lines, they struck me with the force of something I had always known, but somehow forgotten. They are by William Blake, from an unfinished poem called "Auguries of Innocence," about the interconnectedness of all things, and especially the profound connection between faith and truth. To me, they perfectly describe the way a small child sees the world, before she learns to hurry up, settle down, and pay attention to what the grown-ups think is important.

This is the story of a remarkable friendship, which began when I was five years old, and has nourished me all my life.

I have a photograph taken that summer on the platform in Toronto's Union Station. My mother, dressed in a tailored suit of robin's egg blue, is holding my little brother Andrew by the hand. My nine-year-old sister Nancy is in braids and a skirt and blouse. I am wearing a smocked cotton dress and ankle socks, holding my doll, Lazy Mary, by one arm. On the back of the photograph my mother has scrawled the date: June 1963.

We are on our way once again from Toronto to Kenora, on Lake of the Woods. Our train is called the Trans-Canada Limited, or "The Fastest Train Across the Continent."

Once inside the car, we pressed our faces to the window to watch as the train pulled out of the station and began to pick up speed. The little houses became a blur, and then there were green fields all around.

We played beneath the dome of the Observation Car, as the train plunged through corridors of pink granite, over cataracts and sunlit rivers, deeper and deeper into the boreal forest. Sometimes we stood at the back of the train, watching the tracks spool away from us into the far distance, hypnotized by the rhythm of the present becoming the past—Now . . . Now . . . Now . . .

We ate supper in the Dining Car. The table was covered with heavy white linen and there were little silver dishes of olives and celery and cold butter curled into barrel shapes. On the way out, if no one was looking, Nancy would pick up the big silver bowl of multicoloured mints and empty it into her skirt. Then we would make our way back to our room, my sister clutching her skirt to her waist as she lurched down the narrow aisle.

Next morning, in our bunks, we woke to see Lake Superior speeding by.

And then, after another day and another sleep, we arrived at the little station in Kenora. With shaky legs we climbed down the stairs onto the platform. And there was my father, beside the family station wagon with my two older brothers, Sandy and Patrick, and our poodle, Celeste.

Kenora, *née* Rat Portage, was at that time a rugged little pulp and paper town, with a Mill that blew a whistle every day at noon, a little brick Courthouse and a Post Office with a clock tower where we got our mail.

We left the station wagon in the parking lot at Cameron's Point. Dragging our suitcases, we lumbered down the old cracked steps, beneath a canopy of leaves. And then, with a shock of pure joy, we saw it: The Lake—unbearably bright, slapping against the dock in ecstatic welcome.

The boat ride seemed to take forever. When we arrived, we had to stay seated while my father cut the engines and manoeuvred the boat into the echoing boathouse. And then the bags and the dog and the cat in his cage had to be lifted onto the dock. Only *then* were the children allowed to scramble out and run screaming up the hill to the house.

The terraced steps that wound up the hill were covered with pine cones and sticks that crunched beneath our feet. At the top of the hill was one last hurdle—the ten green steps up to the porch. The screen door slammed and the little glass wind chimes stirred in the breeze. Inside the house, the long silence of the winter months hung in the air.

And now began the ritual of arrival. The doors to the living room were swung wide, while my father stood by with a broom in case a bird came swooping down. The sheets in the linen closet were hung outside to air. In the kitchen, the cupboards were flung open and we stood still a long moment, fingers pressed to lips, listening for mice. Then the tins of sugar and flour were taken up and tapped before opening, and the shelves wiped down with hot soapy water.

Upstairs, my mother found a little nest of cotton balls in the medicine cabinet. And then, having cleaned and swept and scoured and thinking we had the place back to ourselves, the screams of Paulina, our nanny, brought us all running to see the dead snake curled up in the waterless toilet.

Otherwise, everything was just as we had left it: the comic book lying open on the couch, last year's swimming chart curling from the wall, a pair of dusty yellow shorts hiding under the bed. And I would always stop to look out the bedroom window at the lake, imagining it in winter, blanketed in snow.

My family was a large one. My mother had been widowed at a young age with three children. A few years later she met my father—then 47—and they had two more.

Sandy and Patrick—"The Boys"— were inseparable, united by their love of mischief and horseplay. They were a constant trial to my sister Nancy, who had the middle child's fierce hostility to injustice. In kindergarten, for example, she had hit an interfering nun on the knee with a small hammer and had to be expelled. Her passions were Mozart and Beethoven and the kings and queens of England.

My younger brother and I were known as "The Littles"—until we were well into our teens. Andrew, at three, was tow-headed, ropy-legged and two-fisted. His first words were "I won't," and from then on he delivered his opinions in a voice that, though high-pitched, was unwavering in its confidence.

I was marked down at an early age as the "sensitive" one. My first report card—from the Happy Days Nursery School—expressed concern over my "excessively emotional" nature. Patrick, less charitably, dubbed me "The Fastest Cry in the West."

My mother tried very hard over the years to cure me of this disabling sensitivity. She feared that I lacked the necessary toughness for life in the "R.W." (her own shorthand for the *Real World*). Once, while I was in the middle of an episode, she held out a goldfish bowl. Smiling, she delivered the punchline: "It's a pity to waste those salty tears—let's save them for the fish!" (Apparently, she had read a magazine article that recommended this "laughing cure" as a remedy for melancholy children. I must have been a particularly hard case, for it had the opposite effect on me.)

My father at this time had recently retired from public office, after a highly publicized and principled battle, to which he never referred. The exact nature of his present occupation remained one of the great unsolved mysteries of our childhood. There was always some inviolable corner of the house to which he would retire after breakfast to pore over his *important* papers. From time to time we would hear him whistling some ancient air from his youth. Later in the day, he would sit in his chair on the porch and do the cryptic crosswords, or read thick books on science or mathematics.

When we had finished opening up the cottage, and had been for our first swim in the cold lake of early summer, on that day or the next it would be time to revisit all our favourite wild places: Blueberry Mountain, and Waterlily Bay, and Spy Point, and the beaver dam, and the marsh where the bulrushes grew.

And then it was time to go and see the Moirs, who lived next door in a modest grey bungalow, with a pine-cone strewn lawn sloping down to the lake.

Mr. Moir's garden was a kind of miracle in the wilderness, nurtured over many years in thin soil and rocks and in spite of the harsh climate. At this time the peonies would be in bloom and the branches of the lilac heavy with flowers. Later in the summer there would be delphiniums and foxgloves, sweet peas and columbines and a profusion of day lilies. There was a stand of raspberry canes, and raised beds of lettuce, rhubarb, squash, tomatoes and corn. Near the water was a large and reeking mulch pile.

When I was small, I spent a part of every day visiting with Mr. Moir, helping him with his tasks and learning from him about plants and animals and much else besides.

Mr. Moir had been a high school inspector on the Prairies during the Depression, working in remote areas of Saskatchewan, travelling by train and horse-drawn carriage. Upon retiring, he and Mrs. Moir had moved to Kingston, Ontario, to be near their son.

He was in his seventies now, a stooped figure in faded flannel trousers. He wore a hearing aid, and a big floppy hat to cover his bald pate. He carried a cane because of a childhood bout with polio that had shrivelled his leg. This disability seemed hardly to trouble him. It certainly did not prevent him from pushing his wheelbarrow deep into the surrounding woods, or from mending the dock, or chopping wood.

When we gardened, he would simply pull himself along the ground as he worked.

Mrs. Moir was a small woman with very pale skin and bright black eyes. She suffered from chronic ill health. Her manner was soft and gentle, like someone from another century, as was her way of dress—long skirts and high-neck blouses. Once a week the Moirs went into town in their canoe to exchange their library books. Mrs. Moir always sat in the bow, holding a parasol in her gloved hands.

Between our two cottages, running down to the little bay, was a thick hedge. Soon after we arrived that summer I was five, I discovered a strange relic there: an old stone fireplace, half-hidden beneath the leaves. Moss and lichen clung to the rough-hewn stones in patches of black velvet and scaly grey, and brilliant dots of mustard-yellow.

I asked my father about it, as he sat on the porch with his crossword puzzle. He looked up. "Well, that's Uncle Joe Spondoolak's house," he said, and went back to the crossword. "Who's that?" I asked. My father put down his pencil. "Well . . . he was an elf, or so they say. There used to be a cottage there and when that burned down only the fireplace was left. And then Uncle Joe moved in and made it into a home for bachelor elves . . . Long time ago, of course." And that was all I could get out of him.

I went back to the fireplace and knelt down to look inside. Deep in the shadows of the cool interior any number of doors might be hidden. I could almost hear the hum of busy elvish lives.

So I started leaving little gifts there for the elves: handfuls of wild strawberries, a daisy chain. And, overnight, the gifts would disappear. I found a little whisk broom and swept the hearth, and I filled some hazelnut shells with water for the elves to drink. And I drew a picture of myself and left it under a rock. These things, too, disappeared.

And then one morning, as I was on my way to visit Mr. Moir, I found something waiting for me. It was a neatly folded piece of pink paper, wedged in between the mossy stones. I turned it over and over in my fingers. Its edges were stuck down with a round seal of wax, stamped with an "N." And on the outside were some words, written in ink in a spidery hand, a little blurred by the dew.

I ran to find Paulina. She was in the laundry room, feeding sheets through the ringer. I waved the paper at her and shouted over the noise, "I found it on the fireplace! What does it say? What does it *say?*" She wiped her hands and took it from me, peering at the inscription: "Not to be opened by any but Susan Coyne." She gave it back and I broke the seal. And then Paulina read me what was written inside:

To Helen Susan Cameron Coyne:

Greetings.
Her Majesty, Queen Mab, has instructed me
to thank you for making a home for all her
people.

The great people—the fairies, the sylphs,
the kelpies, the nymphs, the dryads and
hamadryads—thank you.

The little people—the gnomes, the nixies,
the kobolds, the brownies, the leprechauns,
the elves, the pixies, the trolls—thank you.

I, Princess Nootsie Tah—Little
Hummingbird—granddaughter of Nuitziton,
the Hummingbird, who ruled all Peru, am
banished from my home because people said I
was proud. For a thousand years I may not
go back to my high hills, but must tell boys
and girls who are kind to the great people
and the little people about the fairies—

Oberon and Ariel, Mab and Titania,
Lob-Lie-by-the-Fire and Puck.

I am very beautiful and a great
princess; I am very proud, but it irks me,
Susan, it irks me extremely when people
forget how great and beautiful I am, so
when you talk about me, call me Princess.

The above has been dictated but not
read by Her Serene and Illiterate Highness,
whose seal is attached.

Nootsie Tah
Princess

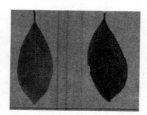

Paulina looked up as she finished the letter. There was an odd expression on her face. "Well," she said at last, "why don't you show your mother and father?"

I ran to find them. My father was reading a book. I stammered out my news, waving the letter in front of him. "Hmmm?" he said, as he looked it over briefly. "Hamadryad, eh? . . . Greek for wood nymph, I believe. Very nice, dear." And went back to his book.

My mother made more of a fuss. "Isn't that *wonderful*? Be sure and write a thank-you letter," she said, as she kissed me goodbye and took off in her motorboat for her tennis lesson.

My sister was playing the piano in the living room, her face intent on the Mozart piece in front of her. I watched her a moment, hesitating. She'd recently offered to cut my dolls' hair and had then shaved them bald. I decided not to show her the letter.

Patrick and Sandy were inside the boathouse, standing on the wooden deck of the Thompson and pointing to where a muskie had just been seen lurking amongst the weeds. "I have a letter here to me from a fairy princess," I said. They looked at each other. "Wow," said Patrick, finally.

"Do you want to see it?"

"Uh, maybe later, okay?"

And they lowered their bacon-laden hooks into the murky water.

I didn't tell Andrew. It wasn't his age so much as his attitude—no one was going to pull the wool over his eyes. When adults tried to talk to him about Santa Claus, or the Easter Bunny, he would give them such a piercing look they would trail off in embarrassment.

So I took the letter to Mr. Moir, who was weeding in his garden. He put down his trowel, took off his gloves and gently took the letter between his bumpy fingers. After a moment he looked up at me and smiled. Hand in hand we went into his cottage, into the inner room with the pot-bellied stove, where the walls were covered from floor to ceiling with books. There, he took down a dusty old volume from the Encyclopaedia Britannica and leafed through it until he found a picture of a dark-haired and bearded man, with flashing eyes. He told me it was Oberon—the King of the Fairies. I was surprised because he didn't look tiny at all. And then Mr. Moir read the words inscribed beneath the picture, a kind of spell, it seemed:

I know a bank whereon the wild thyme blows,
Where oxlips and the nodding violet grows,
Quite overcanopied with luscious woodbine,
With sweet musk roses, and with eglantine:
There sleeps Titania sometime of the night,
Lull'd in these flowers with dances and delight;
And there the snake throws her enamell'd skin,
Weed wide enough to wrap a fairy in.

We looked at the picture for a long time. "What do those words mean?" I asked. And he explained to me that wild thyme was a sweet-smelling wildflower, that violets were a kind of pansy, and that musk roses were a little like our dog roses that bloomed in the hedgerow. He talked about the snake, and I remembered the filmy white skin we'd once found on Blueberry Mountain.

A picture took shape in my mind, as he spoke, of a moonlit night, of the slopes beside the old road that the islanders use in winter, of a faint breeze stirring in the shadows, and a fairy queen sleeping on a moss-covered rock. He finished, and I smiled and nodded. "I'll come back tomorrow, Mr. Moir. And I'll tell you if I get any more letters."

All night I dreamt of the stone fireplace and its inhabitants. When I woke up it was early morning. I ran downstairs and banged out the screen door. Down at the shore, a startled blue heron took flight, flapping its lazy wings over the glassy water.

I raced over the wet grass to the fireplace. The letter, this time, was wrapped in foil to protect it from the dew. It, too, was written on pink paper sealed with wax, and bore the same inscription in the same spidery hand: "This seal not to be broken by any but Susan Coyne." I ran into the house to the back bedroom where Paulina slept, and I made her read it to me as I stared up at her creased and bleary face.

To Helen Susan Cameron Coyne:

Greetings.

In this second letter I am instructed to tell you about our fairy queen—Queen Mab. I think that princesses are more interesting than queens, so I shall tell you about Queen Mab later; today I shall tell you about the meeting of the cats on Blueberry Mountain on Saturday night when the moon was full.

The meeting was called to decide whether all cats in Canada should learn French. If all the people in Canada talk French, how will cats know when they are called to dinner? An important meeting.

There were white cats, black cats, brown cats, siamese cats and white, blue and black Persian cats. There was one Manx cat without a tail from over Keewatin way.

Most of my family can turn themselves into any animal, but it irks me, Susan, it irks me almost to tears that whatever animal I try to be I turn out to be a cat. Saturday I turned into a Maltese kitten. I was beautiful.

Tomorrow I shall tell you about the meeting.

Dictated but not read by Her Highness, whose seal is attached.

Nootsie Tah
Princess

I sat for a long time with the letter in my hands, imagining myself a cat on Blueberry Mountain, creeping over the moonlit rocks And then I thought how sad to be banished from one's home for a *thousand* years.

After supper I dictated a response to Paulina, which she wrote down for me on white paper:

Dear Nootsie Tah.
Thank you. Susan Coyne

She showed me the letter. The words on the page seemed meagre to me. So I got out my crayons and drew a picture of a smiling princess in a floaty dress, gesturing in front of a landscape of rolling hills. We left it on the fireplace at dusk.

Next morning came the reply:

To: Helen Susan Cameron Coyne
From: Her Highness, Princess Nootsie Tah

Greetings.
Thank you for your letter and picture. People tell me you are a good and kind girl, and I believe them. It irks me, Susan, it irks me greatly when girls do not say "Thank you" with their whole heart.

I got to Blueberry Mountain easily, though I had changed to a Maltese kitten. I could see like a cat on the dark path but I wore a coronet of one hundred fireflies that flashed one after another around my head. I was beautiful.

At midnight the cat who was in charge called us all around her. She had glasses and a hearing aid, and was dressed in an imitation Persian coat. You could not say that she was from the top drawer; I wondered if she had been born in a house at all.

She told us that the meeting had been called to decide whether all cats should speak French—it might be that their dinner depended on it. There was a program. A cat from over Norman way sang "In Gay Purr-ee." A big cat from Coney Beach started to tell a story about a boy in his house that asked for more Purr-tatoes, but the chair lady stopped him. "We are not amused," she said. The next cat said he had been going to sing a little catch with some friends, but they had forgotten their music.

Just as they were going to vote to speak French, the Manx cat said that "catnip" was the best-sounding word in the world and he wasn't going to change. Then it was proposed that the children learn French. They all looked at me when I said that I thought that children found living in one language hard enough these days. They saw my fireflies and knew that I wasn't a real cat. So they ran away and left me alone on Blueberry Mountain.

Dictated but not read by her serene and illiterate Highness, whose seal is attached.

Nootsie Tah

I had long suspected our cat was living a double life. So many evenings I had watched him slinking into the shadows behind our cottage, his eyes glowing like coals. And then at breakfast there he would be again, mewing at the screen door, as though he were any ordinary household pet.

I went in search of him and found him asleep beside the chimney on the mantelpiece. I held him close and tried to get him to speak. But although his fur smelled sweetly of the forest, his green eyes gave nothing away.

The next day's letter told me more.

To: Helen Susan Cameron Coyne
From: Her Highness, Nootsie Tah, Princess

Greetings.
I am again instructed to tell you about Her Majesty, Queen Mab.
When she goes to parties, she is called Titania. She is usually called Titania.

When the cats saw my coronet of fireflies last Saturday night, they knew that I was not an ordinary kitten. They thought I was a witch's child and ran away with their tails big, and each went "sfft, pfftt" at me. It was cold on Blueberry Mountain, and I could not remember the words that would change me from a little kitten to a princess.

Just when I started to cry, I heard the song that my mother sang to me each night in the high hills at Cuzco. "It is Ariel," I said, and remembered the words, and was a princess again.

When boys and girls want their mother at night, it is Ariel that comes and whispers them to sleep. Sometimes when bad men plan more badness, he talks to them, too, but his voice is not a whisper. Then, it is like thunder. He travels as fast as you

can think. Instead of saying he will do a
thing right away, or bring somebody, he
talks like this:

> Before you can say, "Come," and "Go,"
> And breathe twice and cry, "So, so,"
> Each one, tripping on his toe
> Will be here with mop and mow.

Dictated by her Gracious Highness, whose
seal is attached.

Nootsie Tah
Princess

And so began my instruction. Each morning I would wake up early and tiptoe across the cold grass to the stone fireplace, under the stern watch of the blue heron on the water. And later that day I would discuss my correspondence with Mr. Moir, while we raked the mulch pile, or weeded the vegetable garden or cut flowers for the table. Mr. Moir knew quite a lot about Ariel and Puck and Oberon and others of that tribe.

To: Helen Susan Cameron Coyne
From: Nootsie Tah, Princess

Greetings.

Do you remember Ariel's singing to me when I was a kitten on Blueberry Mountain? Mostly he is invisible, but sometimes he whispers, sometimes he talks with thunder. Today his singing sounded like an organ: "How beautiful must be the mountains whence ye come!" Princesses from the high hills like people to sing to them like that.

Your mother or father will tell you how he worked for the foul witch, Sycorax, and then for the magician, Prospero. They will tell you that when he did not have to work for anyone any longer, he was so glad that he sang this song:

> Where the bee sucks, there suck I:
> In a cowslip's bell I lie;

There I couch when owls do cry.
On the bat's wing I do fly
After summer merrily.
Merrily, merrily shall I live now
Under the blossom that hangs on the bough.

Nootsie Tah
Princess

My mother, who was reading the letter to me, told me something about a marvellous writer, very famous, who had lived a long time ago and written a play about Ariel and Prospero and some other people. It was quite a complicated story. And he had written some other wonderful plays, with lots of poetry in them, that I would read when I was older.

But Mr. Moir had a picture of Ariel in one of his books, lounging in a flower, like I liked to do in our hammock behind the house. "Where the bee sucks, there suck I," he was saying.

Later, in the garden, we saw a pair of bumblebees buzzing around a frilly snapdragon. Mr. Moir picked a blossom and snapped it for me and then held it up to the light so that I could see the nectar at the bottom. We walked a little way along the forest path, looking for other places where Ariel might couch, and found a lady's slipper. I crouched down beside the little pink flower and touched its delicately veined skin, and Mr. Moir showed me how the bees get trapped inside and have to squeeze through the tunnel, and the green pad that dusts the bumblebee's back with pollen before he pops out the top. And then, to my joy, we found a jack-in-the-pulpit, those funny little laddies standing up under their green-and-white striped canopies.

We walked slowly along the winter road down toward Waterlily Bay. Where road meets water, we found a solitary blue iris, and Mr. Moir told me it was the emblem of the Egyptian pharaohs, for whom the three petals represented wisdom, faith and courage. Then we stood awhile in the oozy mud, watching the ripples of wind on the water and breathing in the pleasant stink of the marsh. It had clouded over during our walk, and far off there was a dark grey light in the sky. A storm was on the way.

After supper, as the rain began to patter on the roof, I dictated a letter to my mother and told Nootsie Tah a little of my life. I begged my mother to let me take the letter out to the fireplace. Finally, she relented and helped me wrap it up in plastic and put on my raincoat over my pajamas and my boots over my bare feet. I got soaked anyway.

I lay in bed for a long time listening to the wind as it lashed the lake and the boats straining wildly at their moorings down at the dock, slapping against the water as they rode up and down. I wondered, as I lay there, where Ariel would sleep tonight, and whether it was his voice I was hearing in the storm.

The next morning the sky was low and grey and the lake was still. The wetness and the cloudy light made the colours of the stones and the moss on the fireplace deeper and softer. A fine rain had begun to fall when I went next door to show Mr. Moir my latest letter.

He was sitting in the book-lined inner room next to the pot-bellied stove. Mrs. Moir was not feeling well, he explained. We'd have to speak quietly.

To: Helen Susan Cameron Coyne
From: Nootsie Tah, Princess

Greetings.
Again I have been requested to tell you about Queen Mab, whose party name is Titania. Her husband's name is Oberon. Oberon is a king. There is no fun in being a king. If a king wants to laugh, he hires a jester. Oberon's jester was called Puck.
You go to bed at 7:30; the boys go to bed at 9:30 on the days they go fishing; the

grown-ups go to bed at midnight, when it is almost fairy time. After midnight, the fairies guard people's houses. If Puck guarded your house, he would stand on the verandah steps and say:

"Not a mouse
shall disturb this hallowed house:
I am sent, with broom, before,
To sweep the dust behind the door."

As a guard, Puck is a good jester.
Dictated but not read by Her Highness, whose seal is attached.

Nootsie Tah
Princess

When Mrs. Moir was not feeling well, we would often sit in the inner room and Mr. Moir would take out his copy of *Alice in Wonderland* and read aloud:

After a while, finding that nothing more
happened, she decided on going into the
garden at once; but, alas for poor Alice!
when she got to the door, she found she had
forgotten the little golden key, and when she
went back to the table for it, she found she could
not possibly reach it . . ."

Or he would take down a big book containing the
records of the international chess championships, and
we would choose a match—perhaps the famous
"Evergreen" contest between Anderssen and Dufresne
in Berlin in 1852—and we would play out the game
exactly as it had happened. I always won.

Today, however, Mr. Moir said he was feeling a
little tired, and perhaps I'd better come back tomorrow
when he was feeling better. The next day came the following letter.

To: Helen Susan Cameron Coyne
From: Nootsie Tah, Princess

Vale. Hasta la vista.

It is my duty to inform you that THEY have asked me to stop my informative and delightful letters about the great and the little people for one week.

They say that I should not have turned myself into a Maltese kitten when the moon was full last Saturday night. They say that even if I did turn myself into a Maltese kitten, I need not have gone to a meeting of old cats on Blueberry Mountain. They say that even if I did go to the meeting, I need not have made myself even more beautiful by wearing a coronet of one hundred fireflies; that in these days of DDT, fireflies are getting scarce. They say that if I had to have fireflies, three would have been enough—two headlights and one tail light.

It irked me, Susan, it irked me profoundly to carry on an argument that was lost before I started talking, so I said no more.

Dictated, but not read by Her Highness, whose seal is attached.

Nootsie Tah
Princess

My mother told me that I was not to bother Mr. Moir while Mrs. Moir was not well, and so I stayed at home. The wet weather continued for two days, and I sat at the window and watched the rain flatten the silvery leaves. My older brothers and sister said I was too young to play Risk and Monopoly with them in the living room and my father was reading his books and my mother was decoupaging a table—cutting out pictures of birds and gluing them onto the tabletop— so Paulina showed Andrew and me how to build a house on the porch by turning over all the wicker furniture and covering it with blankets. This amused us for a while, until Andrew started taking the blankets off and sticking his head up through the chairs and I had to give him a little pinch. Then he told my mother and I was sent to my room.

When the rain let up, we were allowed to go with

my mother into Town and sit in a booth in Jackson's Bakery and order a grilled cheese sandwich and a coke.

Another day we went up the lake in the Thompson to see the sailboats race, taking turns with the binoculars as we watched my older brothers struggle to get their spinnaker up, the last of the fleet. Then we had a picnic on an island, and went swimming off the rocks while my father sat in his webbed folding chair and read.

And then there was the affair of the chipmunk.

Our poodle, Celeste, was not what you'd call an "outdoorsy" sort. She was a homebody, a layabout, a bed-dog. Her one form of exercise was a couple of hours of "barking up the wrong tree" at an insolent red squirrel who lived in one of the twin Jack pines next to the house.

The squirrel would crawl down the trunk to within a few feet of Celeste's head and scold her until Celeste began to bark and attempt to climb up to get him. Then the squirrel would scramble to the top of the tree, leap across to its neighbour, slide down that trunk and start scolding her from there. After several slow minutes, Celeste would catch on and move over, and the next round would begin. And though the ordeal was maddening to watch, it seemed to provide both the squirrel and Celeste with a reason for being.

But one day, as we were sitting in the living room after supper, a chipmunk popped up out of nowhere. When Celeste spotted it, all her frustrated instincts were released and there was pandemonium—dog barking, cat on the mantelpiece hissing and spitting, children howling and my father shouting at everybody to leave the room. Finally, Celeste was shut up in the back bedroom and the chipmunk shooed out the door. Afterwards, Celeste underwent something akin to a nervous breakdown and it was some weeks before she returned to the foot of the pine tree to resume her quarrel with the red squirrel.

(Celeste was never the sharpest knife in the drawer, but she was loyal. When she died my younger brother made a memorial plaque out of wood, burning the letters of her epitaph with his magnifying glass, and he nailed it to the trunk of the tree. "In Memory of Celeste," it said, ". . . who was More than a Dog.")

The other notable event that week was a total eclipse. The radio reports were full of warnings not to look directly at the sun, and so Paulina helped us all make little boxes out of paper with which to view the eclipse. We stood outside and watched as the sky became dark, darker than the darkest storm, and the wind dropped and then there was an eerie silence for several minutes. I reached for my mother's hand. And then the sun came back and for some reason we all cheered.

Later, while we were down on the dock, we waved to the Moirs as they went by in their little canoe. Mr. Moir was dressed in a coat and tie and Mrs. Moir carried a parasol. They were going to the library to change their books. "I'm glad Mrs. Moir is feeling better," said my mother.

The next day, another letter appeared.

To: Helen Susan Cameron Coyne
From: Nootsie Tah, Proud Princess

Greetings.

I am permitted to write you again, if I tell you about Queen Mab.

She goes around in a little wagon. The official language of Fairyland tells about it:

Her waggon-spokes made of long spinners' legs,
The cover of the wings of grasshoppers,
Her traces of the smallest spider web;
Her collars of the moonshine's wat'ry beams;
Her whip of cricket's bone; the lash, of film
Her waggoner a small grey-coated gnat . . .
Her chariot is an empty hazel-nut
Made by the joiner squirrel or old grub,
Time out of o' mind the fairies' coachmakers.
And in this state she gallops night by night.

Most Official Language is hard to understand at first—I hope this gives you a clear picture of our dear queen.

What I wanted to tell you about was riding down the shadow of the eclipse with Ariel, telling the little birds not to be afraid—they knew it could not be night, because there were no sunset colours.

Dictated and partially read by Her Royal and simple-minded Highness, whose seal is attached.

Nootsie Tah

"Were you afraid during the eclipse, Mr. Moir?"

"A little."

We were sitting on the porch playing chess. Mrs. Moir was well enough to lie on the chaise and read her book.

"I don't like the dark, do you?"

"Oh, I don't mind it so much any more."

"Look there's a spinner!" We watched as a rusty daddy-long-legs teetered along the edge of the windowsill.

"It's still your turn."

"Yes." Mr. Moir consulted the book on his knee. "Ah yes, bravo Yuri. Here we are. Queen takes Bishop."

"But I'm still going to win?"

"Sadly, yes. Yuri Pastuk lost this game in 1928 and they say he gave up chess altogether to become a monk."

"What do I do?"

"Queen takes Pawn and check . . . 'Lady, you are the cruellest she alive . . .'"

Beside our house there was a yellow birch tree to which I was attached—literally—as a child. When I was very small I was often put out to play on the grassy slope, tethered to this tree to avoid tumbling into the lake. When I returned home that day, I found a quantity of bark on the ground near my tree. With Paulina's help, I made a little canoe out of the sweet-smelling papery stuff, pegging it together with twigs, and that night I left it on the fireplace.

To: Miss Helen Susan Cameron Coyne
From: Nootsie Tah, Princess

   Greetings.
   I am instructed to thank you for the
birchbark canoe. Queen Mab is already
testing swimmers and water-walkers to see
which will make a better team to draw her
new carriage.

   Yours sincerely,
   Nootsie Tah
   Princess

   P.S. I have already told you that I can
change myself only into a cat, because I am
so proud. If you try to be someone else, a
mouse, say, you have to think like a mouse,
act like a mouse, feel like a mouse. How can
a person be proud and a mouse at the same
time? I can only be some animal that is

proud. The elephant is a proud animal, and once I was just about to try to be an elephant when Ariel buzzed around me like a hornet with a sore tongue:

"Elephants are stately proud, not catty proud," he said, so sternly that I wanted to cry. None of the Little Folk dare to turn themselves into elephants.

I was so frightened that I forgot to tell him that princesses don't look their best when they are elephants. I am not all catty proud; I am a little bit stately proud. I am Nuitziton's granddaughter. I am a princess. That's what I should have said to Ariel.

You know that I rode on the shadow of the eclipse with Ariel last Saturday. Birds are such lovely things, beautiful to look at and heartwarming to listen to, but they hide when an eclipse comes and there is no singing. I felt noble and uplifted as I said

*the words of cheer Ariel taught me. I
decided to be a bird. What happened I
must leave for another letter.*

   N.T.

Mr. Moir and I liked to row out to the middle of
Waterlily Bay to gather lilies for Mrs. Moir. We would
grasp the slimy stems of the white and yellow flowers
and yank hard. And then we would drift for a while,
enjoying the sun on our arms, and the quiet hum of
the marsh. Sometimes I sat in the bottom of the boat,
at eye level with the gunwales, and watched the water-
striders skittering along on the water's shiny black skin.

To: Helen Susan Cameron Coyne
From: Nootsie Tah, Princess. Defender of woman's right to use postscripts

Greetings.

Just after your letter was sealed yesterday I remembered what I wanted to tell you.

After Ariel and I rode down the shadow of the eclipse comforting all the birds, I did not feel so proud and it seemed to me that I could turn myself into something besides a cat—maybe a bird. What bird do you guess?

Not a robin, nor a wren, not a gull, nor an eagle—a halcyon, which most people call a kingfisher. Old people tell me that in winter when the days are dark and stormy, she has her nest floating on the sea, and when the eggs are hatching, there is no wind and there are no waves. The calm days are sometimes called halcyon days, kingfisher days.

Well, I said all the words that my teacher had taught me, and waited.

Fairies don't laugh at people. They laugh only because they are happy. So the fairies around me didn't laugh. But they didn't look sorry for me, either; they looked as if they pitied me. Me, a princess!? Do you know what had happened? I was a cat with a peacock's tail! From somewhere up in a tree Puck said, "Proud as a peacock, still," and Oberon did not tell him to be quiet.

There can never be halcyon days for your unhappy

Nootsie Tah, Princess
X (Her mark)

That summer, I was almost ready to swim on my own. My mother tied a rope around my waist and I swam beside the dock while she held the other end and walked up and down. I would look back from time to time to make sure she was still holding on and one day I looked back and she had let go and I burst into tears at what seemed a betrayal. But shortly after that I swam the length of the dock unaided and then I was allowed to be down by the shore without an adult—to wade in the shallow water, or lie on my tummy peering between the boards at the shadowy world under the dock.

Other times I would fall back into the long silky grass, staring up at a sky of burnished blue, listening to the piercing call of the white-throated sparrow: "Oh Canada, Canada, Canada...."

I taught myself to skip backwards, and tried one day to teach Mr. Moir. But he only smiled and shook his head, saying that he had never had much talent for gymnastics.

Mr. Moir and I loved the funny papers—especially Pogo. Pogo was a possum who lived with his friends in the Okefenokee Swamp and spoke an infectious dialect of garbled English. Spectacles were "speckle-tickles," buttercups were "butter cuspidors," caterpillars were "caterpiggles." Mr. Moir taught me the Pogo Christmas carol and I sang it to Paulina when I had my bath:

> Deck us all with Boston Charlie,
> Walla Walla, Wash., and Kalamazoo!
> Nora's freezin' on the trolley,
> Swaller dollar cauliflower, Alleygaroo!"

Unofficial Mail
To: Helen Susan Cameron Coyne
From: Nootsie Tah, Princess, Instructress in astronomy, etc.

Greetings.

I am instructed to advise you that trial runs of the canoe you presented to the Fairies Institute of Applied Science have been made. Both fliers and water-walkers were tried as teams. The en-djinn-eers found no way of adjusting Queen Mab's driving to changes in the wind so that the canoe would pull smoothly, so they decided to use water-walkers, which work very well.

The whole court went on the trial run the day before yesterday at dawn. The djinns swept away bits of fog that were still float-ing on the water. (Extra spiders had been hired to catch as much of the fog as possible before it started out on the lake—you probably are up early enough to see fog caught in spiders' webs. Really they do a very good job, these spiders.) Queen Mab had to touch the water with her wand to make the lake as smooth as a mirror.

A special seat had been made for her; elves had found a great sea lavender flower in Mr. Moir's garden and she had a new dress to match. The team were all black. Going out they were hitched, tandem, in three lines. Coming back four lines fanned out, something like Eskimo dog teams.

The official trip will be tomorrow—New Moon. You will find, Susan, that you will have to know all about the moon if you wish to understand fairies. You will have to know Latin—CRESCO, which means "I get bigger" or "I wax" and DESCRESCO, which means "I get smaller" or "I wane." One begins with C and the other with D. Sometimes the moon makes a C and sometimes a D. When she says C she really means "I get smaller;" when she says D she means "I get larger." You know that women and girls like to fool people by saying just the opposite of what they mean and the moon is very much a lady.

N.T.

There is never an end to the work to be done in a garden, especially one on the edge of the wilderness. Together we toiled, Mr. Moir and I, suffering stoically through our setbacks—rabbits eating the lettuce, blue jays picking off the best of the raspberries. After a long day, we would relax with a glass of homemade lemonade, and, if it looked at all like rain, Mr. Moir would offer me a rhubarb leaf as an umbrella for the journey home.

One day as we were surveying our work, Mr. Moir thought of an idea to ward off evildoers. We would plant a patch of pansies for the fairies, who would bring luck to the garden. So we buried some seeds and patted down the earth and sprinkled it with warm water. Then we went into the Ice House—so-named because of its former use in the days when ice would be taken from the lake in late spring and kept cold there beneath a blanket of sawdust. Now it was a storage shed, cool and musty and full of interesting odds and ends. There was a cracked leather saddle that had belonged to Mrs. Moir's father, Captain George H. Young, the first cottager on the island. And there were stacks of *LIFE* magazines and old books, washboards, stone crocks, and a toaster that you held up to the fire. Gardening implements and Mr. Moir's hand tools were kept there—saws, sanders and drills—which Mr. Moir taught me to use.

We sat on the floor and made a wooden marker together, and we gouged out the letters to read: "Susan's Pansies."

To: Miss Helen Susan Cameron Coyne
From: Nootsie Tah, Princess
 Granddaughter; Nuitziton, the
Hummingbird

 Greetings.
 I am directed to thank you for planting
pansies.

 The man who does all the hack work for
the Little People in this part of the island
doesn't understand how signs should be
coloured. Could you colour some of the letters
in the sign and see that it is put up near
our pansies?

 Nootsie Tah
 Princess

"Mr. Moir, the fairies must have been in the Ice House last night!"

So I painted in the letters, and we varnished it and put it up in the patch.

Later, as I watered the seedlings, we received a sign: behind the shimmering spray, a ruby-throated hummingbird appeared, hovering over our garden.

To: Helen Susan Cameron Coyne
From: Nootsie Tah, Princess

Greetings.

It is my pleasure to advise you that the colours you have chosen for the letters of <u>Susan's Pansies</u> have been approved by the Fairies' Art Council. Jack Frost, who usually isn't interested in summer artwork, blew in from the North and praised the design.

I have been asked to tell you how pleased the Little People are for your help.

Yours sincerely,
Nootsie Tah
Princess

P.S. A vexing thing happened when I started this postscript, Susan. The miserable mortal whom I get to write these letters complained that his job was to look after my official correspondence and not to write long postscripts to short letters. I said to him the very words that Prospero said to Ariel:

"Malignant thing, dost thou forget
From what a torment I did free thee?"
He: No, princess.
I: Thou dost. What happened to your garden first? Speak, tell me.

He: My columbines turned black.

I: Then?

He: The lake swallowed up my lower gardens.

I: Ungrateful mortal, what owest thou to me?

He: Some flowers grow in my garden; birds sing in my garden still.

I: For your obedience, these I promise you again. But if thou more murmurest . . .

He: The princess is as good as she is wise . . .

And now, Susan, he has made me forget my postscript.

N.

One day in early August, my father appeared at the breakfast table to announce that it was time to pick the blueberries. And so we set out for Blueberry Mountain, with our aluminum tins and ice cream buckets. Celeste trotted along beside us, surprisingly cheerful given her general dislike of any form of exercise.

The winter road was overgrown with horsetails and Queen Anne's lace and goldenrod. The heat and the sweet smells and the monotonous buzzing of the crickets slowed our steps. We searched the underbrush for the path to Blueberry Mountain. On a cloudy day, it was almost impossible to find the opening, but when the sun came out it would appear again, as in a fairy tale. And we would always vow to remember next time: the bend in the road and the old tree stump.

We climbed the forest trail, picking our way over the gnarled roots of trees. I lagged behind, silent as a cat.

At last, we came out of the forest onto the heat-soaked rocks and looked out over the tops of the trees to the lake. From far off came the drone of a boat, and then we saw it in the distance, a little dot on the water leaving a white trail behind it. It felt as though we were standing on top of the world.

Nearby I noticed a strange circle of stones and the remains of a fire. A blue-black dragonfly flitted tipsily among the charred logs. I remembered Nootsie Tah's story of the meeting of the cats and I called out for my brothers and sister to come and see. But they were too busy foraging among the low bushes. And so I, too, set to work, tickling the ripe berries into my pail.

Harvesting blueberries is back-breaking work. But once you start, greed gets hold of you and time drops away and you forget to stand up until all your buckets and pots and ice cream containers are full. And then you have to walk very carefully all the way back home so as not to trip and spill your loot.

When we came back Paulina and I made a blue-berry pie. (My mother "frankly detested" cooking. Her repertoire, when faced with a dinner party, consisted of roast beef or ham, scalloped potatoes and tomato aspic. Unless, of course, she'd got a nice chicken pie from Eaton's delicatessen.)

We cut the shortening into the flour until it looked like porridge, and then I sprinkled the ice water on a little at a time and watched as Paulina, with a frown of concentration, took a fork and little by little created a ball of dough. Then we rolled it out and laid it carefully in the pan, crimped it with our fingers and ladled in the blueberries and sugar, the red juice stain-ing our fingers. Another circle of dough was laid on top and pricked and sprinkled with sugar and then we put the whole thing in the oven. And then Paulina gave me the scraps of dough and found me a little tin plate so I could make a pie for the fairies.

I could not have been more entranced if we'd been turning lead into gold.

To: Miss Helen Susan Cameron Coyne
From: Nootsie Tah, Inca Princess, sent from
her home in the high hill of Sacsahuaman,
and now acting publicity director for the
Little People in Canada West

Greetings.
I am directed to thank you for the
blueberry pie. It is the first blueberry pie
offered to the Little People. Though Full
Moon doesn't come till August 5, Queen Mab
ordered a general feast. Eleven gnomes,
fourteen brownies, forty-two elves, a
leprechaun, a troll, five pixies, eight nixies
and three kobolds turned up. I sat at the
head table.
There was a hush when the pie was
brought in on the shoulders of twelve djinns,
but there was a tremendous cheer when King

Oberon cut the pie with a silver knife made especially for this feast by the seven Dwarfs. Even Queen Mab, who is getting just a little bit fat, had two helpings. The leprechaun sent his plate back eight times.

Finally, no one could eat another bite. King Oberon called to Puck:

"Jester, your best joke."

"Yes, sire," Puck said, "but first, I must say, Your Majesty eats like a bird."

"Like a bird, jester? Why, I eat heartily."

"Yes, sire, a peck at a time."

Oberon was very angry—he does not like to be reminded that he takes big bites.

"No more fooling, jester. I want your best joke."

"Yes, sire. But tell me first—what is better than a piece of Susan's pie?"

"Jester, I know nothing better than a piece of Susan's pie. Do you?"

"Yes, sire—two pieces."

N.T.

In the night, Celeste woke everyone up with her barking and my father went all around the outside of the house with a flashlight but couldn't see anything. So he locked Celeste up in the kitchen, where she whimpered and whined until morning.

After breakfast, Patrick took the garbage out to the incinerator. On the way back to the house, he noticed some strange markings on the white walls beside the kitchen. My father examined them and confirmed that they were paw prints, quite possibly a bear's.

It frightened me to think that a bear had come so close to us while we slept. I kept imagining the big animal opening the screen door and shuffling through the kitchen, then climbing up the stairs to my room.

Of course my sister told me I was being silly and that bears don't attack people, that they just like to eat garbage when they can't get enough of their regular food. And then the boys joked that maybe the bears would come after Nancy, and my sister started yelling and my mother had to come in and threaten to "Lower the Boom," if she heard any more squabbling.

To: Miss Helen Susan Cameron Coyne
From: Nootsie Tah, Princess

Greetings.
At breakfast this morning Puck said:
"Sire, I have written some new verses
that I beg you to listen to."
Oberon, the king, did not want to hear
verses. He was already late for the office.
Queen Mab did not want to hear verses.
There were ant eggs to get ready for lunch
and she did not know whether to serve them
Eggs Mayonnaise or Eggs au Beurre Noire.
But Puck started:

"When elf and kobold start to grin
Whose pie is it they're bringing in?
Oh, Susan's.
When Oberon begs for one piece more
Whose pie is it he's asking for?

Why, Susan's.
Though Mab the Queen is gaining weight
Whose pie is on her salad plate?
Yes, Susan's!"

The Queen was very angry. She does not
like people to say she is getting fat. Mark
my words, there will be more trouble in the
palace.

Yours sincerely,
Nootsie Tah
Princess

"Do you think the bear will come back, Mr. Moir?"

"Perhaps he left his paw print to say to other bears
'Do Not Disturb. Pie-making House.'"

To: Miss Helen Susan Cameron Coyne
From: Nootsie Tah, Unhappy Princess

Greetings.

When the nobody that writes these letters
came for his orders this morning I said,
"The princess cannot write Susan this
morning; the princess has a heartache."

The rude mortal said, "The princess ate
six pieces of Susan's pie last night. Her
heartache is only a queen-size stomach ache.
The leprechaun says he has a heartache, and
wants his mother. He has sung 'Mother
Machree' thirty-nine times. All the dogs of
the island have been howling with him since
the twenty-third time. The kobold says . . ."

I have learned that princesses must not
argue with mortals when they are so smug
and have "I-told-you-so" written all over
their faces. I put my finger on his lips and
said, "Stomach ache or heartache, I wish I

could see my mother. If I cannot go to her in the high hills, could she not come to me?"

He shook his head. "Princess, your mother is well, as well as she can be without you. When the thousand years are passed, and you see again Sacsahuaman, your mother will be the first to say, 'Welcome.'"

Then he told me about my mother, Susan.

It is a secret, all this about my mother, but this mortal said he would ask Ariel whether I could tell you, if you did not tell anyone except your mother, your father, Paulina, Andrew, Nancy and maybe Mrs. Moir. Patrick and Sandy should be the first you tell.

If Ariel says I may tell you, I shall write you to-morrow.

Yours sincerely,
Nootsie Tah

I tried to tell them all at dinner, but an argument was raging about the upcoming regatta. Nancy accused The Boys of trying to scare her by making the boat heel too far. Then Andrew spilt his milk and the cat leapt onto the table and my mother shooed everyone out. Except for me, because I hadn't finished yet. I sat at the table alone with an egg timer and the remains of my dinner.

The next day's letter had the words "top secret" typed in red and black three rows deep around the edge of the paper. Instead of the usual inscription, there was this:

WARNING:
READING FORBIDDEN EXCEPT BY
DAYLIGHT, MOONLIGHT, CANDLE OR
ELECTRIC LIGHT OR SOME OTHER FORM
OF ARTIFICIAL LIGHT. READING BY ANY
FORM OF ILLUMINATION EXCEPT THE
ABOVE WILL BE PUNISHED BY LOSS OF
EYESIGHT.

To: Susan Coyne (Miss H.S.C.Coyne)
From: Nootsie Tah, Princess

Greetings.
Ariel says I may not tell you about my
father who was the guardian of the Temple
of the sun and the great buildings of when
the spaniards came to Cuzco more than 400
years ago. He says, too, I may not tell you
why my mother left Fairyland to live in an
indian hut till they let me come back to
her. Neither may I tell you why you may
not talk about her or me with any spaniard.
I am allowed to tell you that she lives
alone on the mountain waiting for me. Once
a year they let me ask about her. Because
she left Fairyland, she gets old like humans
do. Each year she gets more wrinkled and
bent, but Ariel watches over her. Once when
a man came to drive her from the hut,
Ariel changed himself into a huge snake,

and slithered across the man's feet to drink from the cat's dish. Another time a man started talking crossly to my mother. He looked behind him and saw a big black bear (our black bears have white around their mouths) sitting in a rocking chair, smoking a cigar. It was Ariel, but the man didn't know that, and he ran away.

Now people think my mother is a witch. They are afraid of her, and bring her things to eat.

When my mother sees me again, she will change into a young and beautiful fairy, and we shall live together in a New Temple of the sun.

Yours sincerely,
Nootsie Tah
Princess

That night, my parents had a party and I was allowed to stay up later and say hello to the guests as they arrived in their boats. It grew dark and the house filled up with noise and the smell of gin-and-tonics and cigarettes. I sat down behind the door with my doll Lazy Mary, and listened to the conversations. Someone told a story about a teenage boy who'd had an accident in a boat and was knocked into the water, and he'd had to dive deep down under the motor to avoid being killed.

At last I was discovered and sent to bed. I lay there for a long time listening to the gusts of laughter coming from below, staring at the shadows on the wall. When I finally fell asleep, I dreamt of being underwater, looking up at the surface where a boat was turning and turning in smaller and smaller circles above my head.

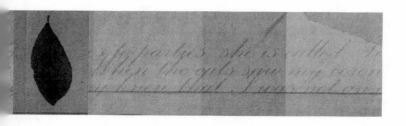

To: Miss Helen Susan Cameron Coyne
From: Nootsie Tah, Princess in exile and trouble

   Greetings.
   I would have gone directly to work this
morning if a grasshopper hadn't jumped this
way and that way—you know how they do—
and I had to follow. He led me straight to a
yellow mushroom in his last jump. Queen
Mab was sitting on it. She had on that
green dress that she wore at the banquet,
not at all what queens should wear out of
doors. She has a way of weaving moonbeams

into her hair that I have tried over and
over again to copy—it would go well with my
black hair; but I can't get it just right. She
whispers nicely, musically, I mean; two or
three octaves of whisper. Have you tried
this?

She said I had to leave Blueberry
Mountain. She said that instead of telling
you the important facts about the Little
People, that would help you grow up, I have
written a lot of tittle-tattle, and wasted
your time for a month. She said she needed
me for another job, north of Churchill somewhere. She said I was to say goodbye to you
as nicely as I could.

Princesses do not often beg. But this
time I begged the queen to let me stay. She
said No. I asked her to let me come back in
a day. No. In a week. No. In ten days. Yes,
if I worked at my new job without nonsense.

So, Susan, you must get along as best you

*can without my help and instruction for ten
days. Your understanding of and respect for
princesses will see you through the difficult
days ahead.*

> *Sincerely,*
> *Nootsie Tah*
> *Princess*

I ran to tell Mr. Moir. He was packing a suitcase
for Mrs. Moir. She had had an attack in the night, and
Mr. Moir was taking her to Winnipeg for some tests. I
helped him carry the bags to the dock and then
watched as he settled Mrs. Moir into the bow of the
boat with a shawl around her shoulders and then put
her parasol into her gloved hands. He pulled the cord
to start the motor and I waved to them until they were
around the corner at Cameron's Point and out of
sight.

Ten days! Every day I asked Paulina, "Is ten days over yet? When will it be ten days? How long is ten days? Is it long till then or short?" Until finally she snapped at me and I went off to sulk.

In a drawer in my mother's room I found a picture of a handsome man I recognized as my mother's first husband who had died. I heard Nancy coming up the stairs and quickly put it back, praying she wouldn't tell my mother I'd been snooping.

I watered my pansies every day, the way Mr. Moir had showed me.

One day, I ventured into the Ice House. Mr. Moir had said I might play there if I did not take down any tools. I stood in the doorway and looked around. It was very quiet and the shadows on the wall and in the corners filled me with an apprehension that I never felt when Mr. Moir was there.

Near the door, I found an old book with drawings in it. On one page I found a picture of a maze, with little fountains and trees cut in funny shapes, and I traced my finger along the path trying to find the way through.

It was a hot afternoon. The air was heavy with the scent of flowers—nasturtiums and calendulas and marigolds. Perhaps I fell asleep, for the air suddenly grew cold, as if a shadow had fallen across the doorway, but when I looked up there was nothing there. Far off, I heard Paulina calling me, an edge of anxiety in her voice. I ran home.

The next day, the Moirs came back from Winnipeg. Mrs. Moir had been given some new medicine and looked a little stronger. She was able to sit out in the sunshine and watch us as we worked.

Later, I showed Mr. Moir the book with the maze and he read me the old rhyme beneath the picture, which began:

> This is the Key of the Kingdom,
> In that Kingdom is a city;
> In that city is a town;
> In that town there is a street;
> In that street there winds a lane . . .

and ended:

> Street in the high town;
> Town in the city;
> City in the Kingdom—
> This is the Key of the Kingdom.
> Of the Kingdom this is the Key.

It was a riddle, telling you that the way out of the maze was to go back the same way you came in.

To: Miss Helen Susan Cameron Coyne
From: Nootsie Tah, Princess

Greetings.

I have been instructed to advise you that in two or three well-written letters it is my duty to make you fully acquainted with all the worthwhile people in Fairyland. I shall begin with Queen Mab.

The official history says:

"she is the fairies' midwife"

This means that she must be present when a fairy is born. If she cannot be there to say, "What a lovely baby!" the new fairy may turn into a gremlin.

Yours faithfully,
Nootsie Tah
Publicity Director
Canada West

P.S. The woman who invented the postscript should have a monument in her honour. Now I can tell you the important news. My trip to Churchill was, of course, secret, but someday I shall tell you about two unpleasant persons I met—Oaf and Loaf. It irks me, Susan, it irks me sorely, that there are parts of your country that do not honour princesses.

The exciting news happens to be about a book in Mr. Moir's ice house. Half a dozen nixies were looking at the queer things he has there, when one of them found a black-covered book that looked so important that they took it to the Grand High Egg Head himself. After reading it for two days, he called the scribes together:

"Scribes, you will gather at the scriptorium at two o'clock tomorrow. Information important to fairies and to Susan has come to hand."

These scribes are called Waterman, Sheaffer and Scripto. I shall tell you more about them tomorrow.

N.T.

"What's a scribe?" I asked my mother, as she struggled to hang on to the doorknob to Andrew's room. My brother was being detained for non-cooperation, and she was determined to make sure he served his time.

"Someone who writes things down for you," she said, between gasps.

"Like Paulina does for me?"

"Yes, dear . . . STOP THAT AT ONCE."

Andrew was now banging murderously on the door, screaming to be let out.

"I want to write a letter myself. Can you help me?"

"Not *now,* dear, " she said with irritation. And then she spoke fiercely to the door, "Now you just settle down, young man. You're going to stay in there until I say you can come out and I want to hear no more noise or there'll be Real Trouble."

At this Andrew began to wail. I shouted at him that he was a gremlin and my mother's eyes flashed fire so I scurried down the steps, away from the field of combat.

To: Helen Susan Cameron Coyne
From: Nootsie Tah, Publicity Director,
Fairies International,
Canada West Division

Greetings.
Continuing my description of our useful
and hardworking Queen, I quote from the
official history:

"She is the fairies' midwife, and she comes
In shape no bigger than an agate-stone
On the forefinger of an alderman,
Drawn with a team of little atomies
Athwart men's noses as they lie asleep:
Her waggon-spokes made of long spinners'
    legs . . ."
But I have told you this before.

Yours respectfully,
Nootsie Tah
Princess

P.S. Yesterday, Susan, I told you about the three scribes: Waterman, Sheaffer and Scripto. The scribes are as old as the great scholar Egg Head, himself. They are so wise that every one of their wishes comes true.

When they were seated at their desks (Waterman had blue paper in front of him, Sheaffer, pink and Scripto, white), Egg Head dictated:

"While exploring the interior of Mr. Moir's ice house, six of the Little People made a discovery that, we think, partly explains Susan's excellence as a cook. In 1896, while Victoria the Good, great-grandmother of Queen Elizabeth, ruled over the land, the Ladies' Aid Society of Grace Church, Winnipeg, wanted to help Winnipeg in the best way they could. They published what they called a Souvenir Cook Book. In that book we found three recipes supplied by a

Miss Mabel Elliott. Our research department
soon found that this person was no less than
a great-aunt of our own Susan. We propose to
make a copy for the use of our cooks and to
offer to Susan a copy, trusting that such a
gracious person will accept it."

N.T.

My father was very surprised to hear that his aunt
was a famous author.

"Mabel Elliott?" my mother called out from the dining room. (She was painting a screen with her favourite
motto: "You can't Stop the Birds from Flying over your
House, but you can Stop Them from Building a Nest.")
"Mabel Elliott's name is on the ceiling in here. Come
and I'll show you." And, sure enough, there it was,
scratched deep into the beam. My father said that Mabel
must have done it when she had visited this cottage as
a girl, more than seventy years before.

To: Miss Helen Susan Cameron Coyne
From: Nootsie Tah, Proud Inca Princess

Gracious Greetings.
I am directed by Ariel himself to tell you
how Mab, our Queen, appeared to one man:

Behold the chariot of the Fairy Queen!
Celestial coursers paw the unyielding air;
Their filmy pennons at her word they furl,
And stop obedient to the reins of light.

He saw our Mab; to-morrow I shall tell you
more of that.

Yours sincerely,
Nootsie Tah
Princess

P.S. I told you yesterday that Egg Head
got the three scribes together to write out

recipes that made your great-aunt's fame as
a cook. Now he began to tell them what to
write:

"Scribe No. 1, Waterman, write:"
"Reverend sir, I write."
"Three cups of brown sugar . . ."
"Scribe, No. 2, Sheaffer, write:"
"Reverend sir, I write."
"Two cups of white sugar . . ."
"Scribe No. 3, Scripto, write:"
"Reverend sir I—, drat this pen! I wish it
were in Toronto . . . One moment, Reverend
sir, till my pen comes back from Toronto."
"Scripto, how often have I told you to
watch your wishes. It is a privilege given to
few to have all their wishes come true."
"Reverend sir, yes, sir, I wish . . ."
"Scripto!"

"Reverend Sir, I write, I mean."

"Beat well the whites of two eggs. Scribe No. 1, write:"

"Reverend Sir, I write."

"One cup of water . . ."

And so they got through the recipes.
This will explain the blot on Scripto's sheet.

N.T.

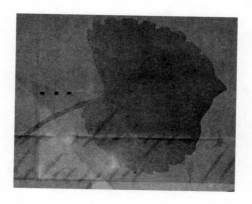

Mr. Moir and I scraped the old paint off the Ice House. I confided in him, as we worked, about the picture I had found upstairs of my mother's first husband.

"You're old, aren't you, Mr. Moir?"

"Very old. As old as the hills."

"Not that old," I said.

"No," he conceded. "Not quite."

"But older than Daddy?"

"Oh yes."

I studied the paint-flecked grass for a moment, considering this.

"Will you die soon?"

"I hope not."

"Well, anyway," I said, looking up, "I'll be sad when you die." And then, "I have new flip-flops, did you see?"

To: Miss Helen Susan Cameron Coyne
From: Her Serene and Happy Highness,
Nootsie Tah, Princess, etc.

Respectful Greetings.
I am commanded to postpone the helpful
and interesting lessons that have been the
subject of all my previous letters and leave
further references to Queen Mab and her
court for a later date. The discovery that
your great-aunt had left us recipes that
would add to the joy of eating stirred
Fairyland as nothing had done before.
The elves called for Maple Cream, the
pixies wanted Peanut Taffy, the kobolds
were all for Dark Creams, the gremlins, who
knew they did not deserve candy, walked
from mushroom to toadstool calling:
"Cavities! Cavities! Remember your
cavities!" No one listened to them.

Finally Queen Mab said, "The Queen is pleased to order that at two o'clock the royal kitchens will be opened for candy-making."

From nine o'clock on there was a steady stream of carts pulled by the strongest beetles bringing sugar, eggs, vanilla, butter, dates, and all the rest to the palace. The elves, the pixies and the kobolds were to do the cooking, but who could stay away? Gnomes, djinns, bogles, nixies, brownies, leprechauns were everywhere. The brownies had brought the brownie baby, Aguecheek, who sat on the floor, rocking back and forth, saying, "Thoon! Thoon!!" I said to him, "Not Susan, Susan's great-aunt." But he only laughed and said, "Thoon, thoon." Don't be cross with him, Susan. He is so little.

There was some trouble with the Maple Cream. The master cook was working his eighteen stirrers to their very limit. The recipe that he had on his desk in front of

him said "stir until thin." The stirrers weren't getting much thinner, and the candy was getting thicker. No one knew what to do. Finally they called in Egg Head. He found that the scribe had written "thin" where it should have been "thick."

Nothing else happened, nothing you'd be interested in. One of the pixies wrapped a peanut skin around himself and pretended to Aguecheek that he was a real peanut. A stone from one of the dates slipped from its chains and crashed to the floor, just missing Aguecheek.

By six o'clock, there were piles of candy cooling everywhere in the kitchen and all the pots and pans had been washed and hung up in their places. I hope Queen Mab will have the party soon—the next full moon is so far away. Even Ariel, who, you know, feeds on honeydew like the bees, may be there.

Yours sincerely,
Nootsie Tah
Princess

I found some of Nancy's paints in a drawer in her room and I made a picture of the candy-making. I showed it to Mr. Moir before I gave it to the fairies.

To: Miss Helen Susan Cameron Coyne
From: Nootsie Tah, Princess

Greetings.

I am directed to thank you for your drawing left at the Hospice for Uncle Joe and the Elves. Jack Frost again came down from the North to see it. (You can usually tell when he has been around by the cold next morning.) He and the committee were pleased with your work.

Yours respectfully,
Nootsie Tah
Princess

Dictated and the words of one letter read by Her Serene and Knowledgeable Highness, whose seal is attached.

P.S. Susan, have you noticed the new seal which I am now permitted to use? Ariel brought it.

It is my mother's.

Once the handle was of pure gold set with emeralds, rubies, turquoises and diamonds. The Spaniards took the handle and threw the seal away. How it was returned to my mother, I cannot tell you. The seven Dwarfs made a silver handle for it, with silver beads instead of the priceless jewels.

It is given to me because of my work at Churchill and the excellent lessons I have given you. The chief superintendent of Erudition said that never before had one of my intelligence gone so far. Such friendly and almost flattering words are heartwarming. They make me forget Oaf and Loaf—almost.

N.T

It was mid-August. The days were hot and the air was motionless. The Boys were busy with sailing races. Nancy took over the dining room table, where she had a big sheet of paper on which she was devising a coat of arms for herself. When she discovered that her paints were muddied and broken she was furious. I tried to tell her that I had only wanted to do a special picture for the fairies. She called me a baby and said that everybody knew there is no such thing. Then she clapped her hand to her mouth. I stared at her, unable to speak, and then ran to my father on the porch.

I told him what she had said and asked him if it was true that there were no such thing as fairies. He didn't answer right away, but looked up out of the cor- ner of his eye, following the progress of a spider creeping along the screen. Then at last he spoke. "Well, I would say that based on the research you have done, and the evidence collected, a reasonable argument can be made for the existence of fairies at Lake of the Woods. I should therefore ignore the scoffers, as many famous scientists have done in similar circumstances."

And then he returned to his book.

Later that day, Paulina and I and Andrew walked across Coney Island to the public beach on the other side. We played "Alligator" in the shallow water.

It was my mother's turn to have the ladies in for an afternoon of bridge, and afterwards they all went down to the dock and sat in deck chairs with their Dubonnets-on-ice, talking and laughing.

Patrick lost a tooth. He didn't believe in the tooth fairy any more, so I begged him to give it to me. My mother said I must clean up the mess I had made in the living room before she would help me with the letter. She reminded me that fairies don't like untidiness.

Dear Nootsie Tah,

This isn't my tooth but it is Patrick's tooth. He gives me his old teeth for the fairies. I hope you need one. Thank you for all your letters. I am trying to be a good girl.

P.S. Dictated but not read by Susie.
/mc

To: Miss Helen Susan Cameron Coyne
From: Nootsie Tah, Princess, Agent, Fairies Federation, Division of Canada West.

Re: Molar 937X18y537M42
   I am directed to advise you that this molar, listed on our books to be delivered to Division of Canada East, Toronto Section, September 14, was received at the Hospice of Uncle Joe and the Elves yesterday.

Teeth are usually sent in by placing them under rugs. Your name is so well known, however, that the committee passed on the tooth for payment, even though it had been placed <u>on</u> a rug.

Since the amount enclosed is to be charged to Canada East, you are asked to sign the enclosed receipt and return it within three days.

Yours, etc.,
Nootsie Tah
Business Executive
Dictated in haste by her Zealous and Executive Highness, whose seal is attached.

P.S. The unexpected arrival of this molar has upset the Federation even more than my wearing one hundred fireflies to a meeting of old cats.

You must understand that Grumpy of

the seven Dwarfs became even grumpier
after Snow White left. He came West, and
became treasurer of our section of fairies.
Even King Oberon finds it hard to get his
bills paid since Grumpy came. The treasure
house doors are rusty and cobwebby.

When I brought 937X18y537M42 to him,
he said:

"Go away, girl." (Even princesses are
merely girls to him since he met Snow
White.) "Go away. No teeth are to be
received today. Anyway, it's likely an adult
permanent. You know we don't take these."

"This is 937X."

"Nothing to do with me. Take it to
Canada East."

"This tooth was sent in by Susan Coyne."

"Our Susan Coyne?"

"Yes."

"Well, why didn't you say so before? Don't
stand there like a lampstand. Get moving."

The treasure house doors squealed as we opened them. Grumpy kicked aside a bag of pearls and threw two or three rubies back into the ruby bin, grumbling about careless help. He took a nickel from the five-cent bin, crossed off 100,301,542 and wrote 100,301,541 and handed the nickel to me.

I said, "Thank you."

He said, "Get a receipt."

N.T.

The vegetables in Mr. Moir's garden were ripening. There were fat zucchini hiding under the thick green leaves, and tiny little carrots that tasted like candy, and pale green lettuces. We were in doubt whether the tomatoes would have survived the recent cold snap, but they were still there, with a soft blush of red over the green.

We sat on the little porch behind the kitchen shelling peas and I taught Mr. Moir a song I had learned at my Unitarian Sunday school (Unitarians, as someone once remarked, believe in at *most* one God):

> Il était une bergère
> Et ron ron ron
> Petit pa-ta-pon.

And Mr. Moir said, "That's odd. I heard a little voice singing that song the other day when I was in the Ice House. Could it have been Grumpy, I wonder?"

"Do you go to church, Mr. Moir?" I asked.

"We go to the Sydenham Street United Church in Kingston." And then he taught me a poem he had learned from his Scottish grandfather when he was a boy:

> Wha's my Shepherd, weel I ken
> The Lord himsel's is He.
> He leads me where the girse is green
> An' burnies quate be.
>
> Aft times I fain astray wad gang
> An' wanner far awa'.
> He fin's me oot, He pits me richt
> An' brings me hame an' a'.

His guidness an' his mercy baith
Nae doot will bide wi' me,
While faulded on the fields o' time,
Or a' eternity.

To: Miss Helen Susan Cameron Coyne
From: Her Serene Highness, Nootsie Tah

Greetings.

I have told you, Susan, that Queen Mab could weave moonbeams into her hair in a way that the rest of us needn't try to copy. Also she whispers in a musical voice. I suppose she learned it whispering lovely words into each fairy baby's ear when it was born. (She _is_ the fairies' midwife.)

I told you, Susan, that one man saw her stop her car and get out to weave a spell about a girl who was sleeping. He told the story in queer words like this:

Oh! not the visioned poet in his dreams . . .
So bright, so fair, so wild a shape
Hath ever yet beheld,
As that which reined the coursers of the air
And poured the magic of her gaze
Upon the maiden's sleep . . .
Those, who had looked upon the sight
Passing all human glory,
Saw not the yellow moon,
Saw not the mortal scene,
Heard not the night wind's rush,
Heard not an earthly sound,
Saw but the fairy pageant,
Heard but the heavenly strains
That filled the lonely dwelling.

He saw her wave her wand, the wand,
you know, that has flowers that do not fade
twined about it:

From her celestial car
The Fairy Queen descended,
And thrice she waved her wand
Circled with wreaths of amaranth;
Her thin and misty form
Moved with the moving air
And the clear silver tones,
As thus she spoke, were such
As are unheard by all but gifted ear.

If Queen Mab makes anyone who sees her
talk like that, it is a good thing that only
a few people have seen and heard her. Of
course, to us fairies, she is rather common-
place. But I wish I could manage moonbeams.

Nootsie Tah
Princess

Each time I passed the old fireplace, I knelt down to look inside, and to touch the damp green walls. Sometimes a butterfly would alight and I would watch without moving while it fanned its pale wings against the dark stones. Or I would follow the progress of a little ant teetering along the stone edge with some strange burden.

I composed a long letter and dictated it to Paulina. "Make sure you use your best writing, *scribe*," I said.

Dear Nootsie Tah, Princess,

I enjoy your letters very much and I thank you for them.

I was born in Ottawa and I live in Toronto. I have some friends named Frannie, Sarah, Carol and Maria. I have got a nice little doll with a party dress on it. I am going to Brown School next fall for kindergarten. Greetings—I get popcorn from the pop-corn man on Fridays.

I like the big "N" on your seal. I hope you write some more letters with the big "N" on them. I have hot dogs most of the time when I come home from Oriole Nursery School. I have a lot of dolls in Toronto and on the sidewalks there are piles of snow in the winter. I sometimes go to puppet shows in Toronto but it's always—most of the time though the same one, "Burtle the Turtle." When I went to the Oriole Nursery School I went to the same Sunday school only in a different room. In Nursery School there's lots of toys there like "Sticks and Stones might break my bones" (I'm just saying that for a joke).

We have two wading pools in Toronto only one has a leak. You know, we have a brown house with white on the top with a red roof. I have a green fence and a green gate and a nice, big, huge yard with pavement at the back and you can slide down it with your bike.

I love you very much. I will send you some more letters.

Susan Coyne

P.S. This letter was completely dictated by Miss Helen Susan Cameron Coyne. Also please forgive the poor effort on the part of her scribe.

To: Miss Helen Susan Cameron Coyne
From: Nootsie Tah, Princess

Greetings.
I am directed to write you, thanking
you for your letter telling me about your
lovely home, your friends and your plans for
further self-improvement. Many of the
mothers were impressed with the addition of
hot dogs and popcorn to your diet—good
brain food, both of them, everybody agreed.

Yours with admiration,
Nootsie Tah
Princess
A1 Instructress
Dictated and the easy one-letter words
read by her serene and mind-enlarging
Highness, whose seal is attached.

P.S. Some persons in the fairies general
council say that I have wasted your time

this summer, that I have gossiped the
summer away without telling you anything
about fairies. They say that since I got
through the Churchill job in ten days (which
I did, Susan—I told them all about Queen
Mab in ten minutes, finished with Oberon
the same day, gave two days to Puck and a
week to Ariel), why haven't I done the same
in your case? And so on, and so on, natter,
natter, natter. Your letter stopped their
grumbling. You were satisfied, and nothing
else mattered. Thanks, Susan.

Nearly everybody was at the general
council meeting. Even Aguecheek. All were
especially interested in the Brown
kindergarten you will attend. Everybody was
sure you would do well. They thought that
when the class got to the subject of house
painting, your views on the merits of rotary
sanders and wire brushes would be received
with respect. They expect that you will get

an A in pansy planting. Aguecheek listened to all that was said. "Thoon, bownie?" he asked. I told him that Susan was not going to be a brownie, that Susan was going to the Brown kindergarten. He only hugged himself. "Thoon, bownie," he told me. Really, he is too little to take part in these meetings.

Tell me, Susan, how to get a writer who will write more than one-page letters? The one I have won't even turn the page over.

N.T.

One day, the wind shifted and the air carried the cool scent of autumn. Overnight, little scraps of bright colour appeared among the leaves.

We went up the lake through Devil's Gap to Forrest Island, which my father had purchased in his bachelor days. It had a one-room cabin that he had built himself, and a little hut that housed a generator for electricity, and an outhouse.

When we got there, the grass was over my head and I watched in fascination as my father—in his casual dress of a *short*-sleeved oxford-cloth shirt and grey flannels—cut it down with an iron whip. After lunch, while my brothers read comic books in the cabin, I went for a skinny dip off the narrow dock. The water was colder there, and the ladder was covered with soft green seaweed, like mermaid's hair. And then I dried myself in the sun, like a turtle on a rock.

Later in the day we took a walk around the coast of our little dominion, visiting in turn all the special places that my mother had named: Boule Rock, Stagnant Pond, the Old Steps and the little bower called Goblins' Grotto. At Pirate's Cove we climbed over the rusted remains of an old ship. On Sunset Point we watched the sun begin to sink behind the dark silhouette of the forest.

Far out from shore, a solitary loon drifted mournfully on the water. My father astonished us all by cupping his hands and calling out to him. We held our breath. Silence. Again my father called and before he had finished came the reply wavering across the water, plangent and full-throated.

Further on, we came across an ancient and twisted Jack pine clinging stubbornly to the rocks. My father told me about its cones, which remain on the tree for up to twenty-five years, tightly closed, sealed in resin. Only the tremendous heat of a forest fire can force them open and release the seeds inside.

We sank down in the deep moss to examine the exposed roots of a storm-toppled white pine. The soft carpet was pierced everywhere with tiny pink flowers. We called that place Fairies' Glen.

By the time we got back to the cabin, the lake had darkened to the colour of quicksilver, and fireflies flickered in the shadows like Christmas lights. We climbed back into the boat. My father let me sit on his lap for a while and hold the steering wheel but soon it got too dark and he needed to shine a flashlight on the buoys that marked the treacherous rocks. I sat in the back with Celeste. The moon spilt its silver light across the water. It was in the shape of a D so I knew it was getting bigger.

The next day I made a little hat out of paper and decorated it with a soft feather we had found on the island. I drew a picture of our outing, and then I dictated a letter to Paulina.

Dear Nootsie Tah, Princess
From: Miss Helen Susan Cameron Coyne

Tell this to Grumpy—I am sorry I didn't give the receipt back too early but here it is now.

We went up to Forrest Island and there is a secret grotto and a Pirate Ship and some of it is still there. And there is lots of moss on one side of the Island and that's where the Fairies live and there isn't any moss on the other side and we think that's where the Gremlins live.

We found this feather way at the end of the Island and I brought it home for you.

We are going home in a little more than a week. Have you noticed the picture I sent you and the Pirate Hat that you can share with Aguecheek? (I hope Aguecheek has a big enough head for it.)

I have rose pyjamas. That's all for now.

Love, Susan

To: Miss Helen Susan Cameron Coyne
From: Nootsie Tah, Princess

Greetings.

I am directed to acknowledge receipt of letters, paintings, a cone, a Pirate Hat and a feather.

The Fairies Federation does not know how to repay you for your many kindnesses.

The pictures are being kept until Jack Frost returns. You will know when that is for the weather man calls him a "cold front" or a "mass of Arctic air." All you have to do is listen to the weather on the radio or TV.

Thanking you for your kindness and generosity.

Yours in admiration,
Nootsie Tah
Princess
Director of Publicity
Fairies Federation
District of Canada West
Dictated but not read by Her Serene and Elated Highness, whose seal is attached.

P.S. Grumpy must have got his receipt, Susan, for he came to breakfast singing that song that Puck sings:

Siffle et sonne,
Tombe et tonne,
Prend et donne
A la mer . . .

Can you imagine Grumpy singing? When he said "tonne," the castle shook.

Your letters make me want to tell you that maybe I am not as beautiful as you think. If you like me, then I do not have to pretend that I am as beautiful as Queen Mab, but I shall try to be. Do you remember what that man said about her,

> "Oh! not the visioned poet in his dreams . . .
> so bright, so fair, so wild a shape
> Hath ever yet beheld"?

Isn't that just like a man to tell us how she looked, not what she wore? I wonder what dress she had on? She has a seersucker that she likes very much, maybe that was the one. I think I'll get a seersucker.

N.T.

The sunflowers in Mr. Moir's garden were well over my head, and almost over his.

To: Miss Helen Susan Cameron Coyne
From: Nootsie Tah, Princess, Director

Greetings.

I am directed to inform you that there are gremlins on Forrest Island. The FBI (The Fairies Board of Informers) believe that they have been there since the wreck of the Pirate Ship.

The Fairy Council could not decide what to do with the feather and the Pirate Hat. They would like your help in deciding. Aguecheek could hide under the hat. He is so

hard to look after now that the council
would rather not leave the hat anywhere
near him.

Yours sincerely,
Nootsie Tah
Publicity Director
(By order of Her Highness, her royal
rank will not be noted in future letters.)
The seal of the Director is attached.

P.S. There is no news that you would be
interested in, Susan. Of course the castle dog
has been chasing the cat that tried to
catch him when he was a mouse and there
are broken dishes and upset chairs, and
Aguecheek picked up the Queen's second-best
wand that fell from her lap at lunch and
we think that's why the soup turned out to
be ice cream, but the Queen merely said

that we'd have dessert first. Having lunch backwards like that seems to have upset my whole day.

N.T.

Dear Nootsie Tah,

    I went aqua-boarding today.

    It was funny that Grumpy was singing that song:

    "Il était une bergère

    Et ron ron ron

    Petit pa-ta-pon"

    That's the song they are going to learn (the fairies are going to learn).

    Paulina wrote the letter all about my life and where I was born—do you remember? When it's cold days we always put on a fire (she doesn't know that but she knows when I'm bad—but most of the time I'm good).

(and then, in my own printing)
I AM WRITING THIS FOR YOU.
S-U-S-A-N-C-O-Y-N-E—BOOK-LOOK

My mother hated throwing food out and so our meals during these last days of the summer consisted of anything left in the cupboards that wouldn't survive the winter or the mice. This caused some grumbling among the children as we had to have porridge for breakfast and eat brown bananas and green potatoes and strange omelettes. "Perfectly good!" my mother exclaimed.

(Personal note only. No official note taken of contents. J.N. censor)

To: Miss Helen Susan Cameron Coyne
From: Nootsie Tah, Princess

Greetings.

Breakfast is often not a happy meal at King Oberon's. Oberon is usually worrying about the work that is piling up in the office. Queen Mab is usually worrying about what she should have for lunch or, if she is on a diet, what she shouldn't have. Most jesters try to be funny after dinner or at night; Puck tries to be funny, or at least brighter than usual in the morning.

This morning Queen Mab was in the breakfast room alone, when Puck danced in singing a little French song that went something like this:

Le navire est à l'eau
Entends rire ce gros flot
Que fait luire et bruire
Le vieux sire Aquilo

You remember what I told you about Mab:

she is the fairies' midwife, and she comes
In shape no bigger than an agate-stone
On the forefinger of an alderman,
Drawn with a team of little atomies
Athwart men's noses as they lie asleep . . .

Well, you can't drive a wagon over some
kind of noses without breaking something,
and she had broken some spokes on last
night's trip. Spinners' legs aren't easy to
get, and so she was not in a good humour.
"Will you stop that outlandish singing!
Don't you know any English songs? Don't
answer that. Where's His Majesty?"

"Oberon the verandah, gracious queen."
Queen Mab was very angry because of
this silly answer. Oberon wasn't there to
protect Puck, so she tried to throw a spell
over him that would have changed him into
a mouse. He slipped out from under it, and
it fell over the castle hound who turned into
a little mouse that just got into a hole in
the wall before the castle cat caught him.
Queen Mab was very, very angry and threw
another spell that would have turned Puck
into a grasshopper but he dodged again and
it hit the scribe Scripto, who was just
coming in.

It irks me, Susan, that I can't throw a
spell over this man who refuses to write more
than one page. I had so much to tell.

N.T.

We were digging and separating plants, preparing the garden for fall. "We have to go home soon, Mr. Moir, " I said. "Are you going too?"

"We go home a little later, in September. But you have to go back to go to school."

"I wish I didn't have to. I wish I could just hide in the house when everyone leaves and stay here until next summer."

"Wouldn't you be lonely?"

"I'd have Nootsie Tah to keep me company."

"Ah. Yes."

To: Helen Susan Cameron Coyne
From: Nootsie Tah, Princess

Greetings.

Susan, this is a note only. The whole palace seems upset. I think Grumpy started it. It seems a receipt for some money hasn't turned up, and he has been nagging at Oberon about slackness in the post office. Oberon claims that the palace has its fastest runner on the job; all Grumpy says is, "I hate this slow male."

You can imagine that breakfast again was cheerless. The king brightened up a little when Puck came in whistling that French tune he picked up:

Dans l'espace
Du grand air
Le vent passe
Comme un fer

But when he saw Queen Mab was not pleased, he turned his back on Puck and whistled for his hound. You can imagine how surprised he was when a little mouse ran up his leg and licked his face and wagged its tail.

"What goes on here?" the king roared.

Queen Mab turned red; she really had forgotten about the hound and Scripto, the scribe.

Puck said, "Her Gracious Majesty was doing a little spelling before breakfast the other day."

"Why does she have to worry about spelling? What are scribes for? Where is Scripto?" (This is Scripto's duty day.)

A grasshopper jumped onto the table beside his plate.

"Another mis-spelling," Puck explained.

Then the king understood. "My dear," he

said "would you favour us with a little
unspelling?" The queen waved her wand, and
things were back to normal. If they stay
that way for two days, you and I can get
some work done.

N.T.

The time had come to write to Nootsie Tah in my
own hand. I sat at the table on Mr. Moir's porch and
took up my pen. I knew just what I wanted to write
and while Mr. Moir read his book I wrote out the
words. Sometimes I had to ask him for help with the
spelling. Then I folded my letter in three and left it on
the fireplace.

DEAR NOOTSIE TAH,

*THANK YOU FOR YOUR LETTERS. I HOPE
YOU GIVE ME SOME MORE. I LIKE THEM
VERY MUCH.*

I HAVE RED AND BLUE SLACKS.

*I THINK YOU ARE AS BEAUTIFUL AS
QUEEN MAB. I LOVE YOU.*

*ON AUGUST 31 I AM GOING BACK TO
TORONTO. I WILL MISS YOUR LETTERS.
PLEASE WRITE ME NEXT YEAR IF YOU CAN.*

*LOVE,
SUSAN COYNE*

The next day's letter was written on white paper,
instead of the usual pink.

Oberon's Palace
New Moon + 4

Dear Susan,

It gives me such a comfortable feeling to know that you think I am very beautiful. Now I do not have to pretend. It was a little bit silly to use pink paper to write my letters on and to start all my letters with "Greetings." Maybe I should have used only fifty fireflies when I went to Blueberry Mountain.

I have decided to go back to my own simple Inca costume and not wear clothes just to get attention. It would be nice to try moonbeams and seersucker once, though. I never had a mother to help me pick out my clothes.

The palace is a little quieter. The castle dog chased the cat for three days. Anyone can stand two days of cat and dog running through a house, breaking dishes and upsetting

furniture, but Queen Mab and King Oberon
are overhasty, and you could tell at breakfast the way the king looked at the queen
that she would have to do something about
it. So she waved her wand and turned the
dog into a china dog and the cat into a
calico cat, and put them up on the mantel.
She forgot to turn off the sound (or maybe
Aguecheek did something to the wand);
anyway, they are still talking crossly to one
another.

   Thank you, Susan, for your friendly letter.

   Sincerely,
   Nootsie Tah

It was quiet on the lake, too. There were very few boats to be seen. Most of the cottagers had boarded up their boathouses and cottages and pulled the boats up out of the water. The clouds in the sky were very high and very white.

King Oberon's Palace
New Moon + 5

Dear Susan,
It happened on the way to Blueberry Mountain, where I was taking a silver pitcher. You remember that while most people are enduring dog-days, we had three dog-and-cat days. This pitcher was broken on the third day and I was going to the dwarfs to get it mended.

It was a perfect summer day; this made me think of the halcyon days in winter when no wind blows; this made me wish that I were a halcyon, a kingfisher. I wanted halcyon days for you this winter, so I said the magic words.

One minute I was Nootsie Tah, the next minute I was Ceryle Alcyon, with a rough crest and a slaty blue back. While I was sitting on a dead branch watching for minnows, I heard someone calling: "Nootsie Tah! Ceryle Alcyon!" and the echo came back from the swamp "Alcyon!" It was Ariel. When the birds heard this whisper of an echo they came out of the swamp and gathered round my tree to listen.

"Nootsie Tah, Susan says she loves you. Love is stronger than all of Queen Mab's spells. The difference between the fairies and the angels is love. God is love." And all the

birds bowed their heads. "For a time, the
spell that keeps you here is lifted."

I was so frightened that I became
Nootsie Tah again. There was a broken silver
pitcher in my hand, and I was on the way
to Blueberry Mountain.

Was it a dream, Susan?

Nootsie Tah

P.S. I wish I could write my own letters,
as you do.

N.T.

The birds were leaving. Every day now, the sky was full of noisy squadrons of geese heading south. My blue heron had disappeared from the bay.

It was cold in the kitchen at breakfast time and we wore long pants all day long.

Down by the dock, a faded plastic sand pail washed up on the rocks. We picked it up and put it away in the boathouse with the other toys.

On the morning before we were to leave I received this letter:

OBERON'S PALACE
FIRST QUARTER-TWO

MADAM,

THE HACK HIRED TO WRITE LETTERS
FOR THIS OFFICE HAS QUIT, SAYING THAT
WHEN PRINCESS NOOTSIE TAH LEFT, HE
NEED NOT WORK FOR ANYONE ELSE. THE
SCRIBES HAVE AGREED TO WRITE THIS
LETTER FOR ME.

THE PRINCESS LEFT YESTERDAY FOR
CUZCO AND SACSAHUAMAN, THAT HIGH
HILL. NO REASON FOR HER GOING WAS
GIVEN. SHE WAS ESCORTED BY ONE OF THE
GREAT ONES, ARIEL.

BEFORE SHE WENT HIS MAJESTY GAVE
A DINNER IN HER HONOUR. MAPLE AND
DATE CREAMS AND PEANUT TAFFY, MADE
FROM FAMOUS RECIPES OF THE LAST
CENTURY, WERE SERVED.

THERE WAS ONE SONG. PUCK SANG A VERSE FROM MARY BEATON'S SONG;

VOIS, LA BRISE
TOURNE AU NORD,
ET LA BISE
SOUFFLE ET MORD . . .

THE SPEECH OF THE EVENING WAS MADE BY AGUECHEEK. LEANING FORWARD IN HIS HIGH CHAIR, HE SAID EARNESTLY, "THOON, NOOTIE, CHEEK. TAFFY," MEANING: SUSAN LOVES NOOTSIE TAH; NOOTSIE TAH LOVES AGUECHEEK, AND AGUECHEEK LOVES TAFFY.

REGRETTING THAT IT WILL NOT BE POSSIBLE TO CONTINUE YOUR LESSONS,

YOURS TRULY,
ADDIE ADDIEVSKI X (HER MARK)
ACTING PUBLICITY DIRECTOR

I sat on the green swing on the verandah while my mother read the letter out loud. When she finished I sat very still, looking out over the grey water. "Well," my mother said brightly, smoothing out the letter on her lap, "Isn't that nice. Nootsie Tah is going home!" She looked up at me and something in my five-year-old's face caused her to become very quiet and serious. "Because of you, Susie dear. When you said 'I love you' you set her free." I forced myself to look back at her. "If I'd known she was going to go away," I said, choking with feeling, "I'd never have said 'I love you.'" And then the dam burst and it was some time before my mother could calm me down.

I needed to tell Mr. Moir, but my mother made me wait until I'd stopped crying and then I had to promise not to upset him. I ran next door and found him with Mrs. Moir hanging clothes on the line. I held out the letter to him, biting my cheek to keep from crying. And then I told him how I wished I'd never told Nootsie Tah I loved her. He knelt down in front of me and looked in my eyes, his expression very grave.

Then he put his arms around me and we stayed that way for a long time. Hand in hand, we went into the house to the book-lined inner room, and he found the photograph of Ariel sitting in a cowslip, slipped it out of its corner tabs and put it in my hand. And in another part of the book, he found a pressed flower, a blue pansy, for me to remember our garden by.

We spent the rest of the morning putting mulch on the cardinal flowers to protect them from the frost. We had lunch on his verandah and then read the end of *Through the Looking-Glass*. The White Knight sang the song of the Aged, Aged Man, which was so silly I had to laugh.

As the Knight sang the last words of the ballad, he gathered up the reins, and turned his horse's head along the road by which they had come. "You've only a few yards to go," he said, "down the hill and over that little brook, and then you'll be a Queen—But you'll stay and see me off first?" he added as Alice turned with an eager look in the direction to which he pointed. "I shan't be long. You'll wait and wave your handkerchief when I get to that turn in the road? I think it'll encourage me, you see."

"Of course I'll wait," said Alice: "and thank you very much for coming so far—and for the song—I liked it very much."

On the way home I stopped beside the old stone fireplace and knelt down, laying my head on my arms and listening to the hush of the wind in the dry leaves.

And so we returned to Toronto on the train, to the house and the yard and the slide and the popcorn man. I began my formal schooling at Brown School, and life filled up with birthday parties and playing with the girls on my street and skating lessons. Experience soon taught me to keep my fairy story to myself.

I wrote to Mr. Moir of my new life, and in December came this reply:

December 1, 1963

Dear Susan,

How nice of you to tell me about your friends and your dolls and your work at Brown School. You seem to be as busy and happy as you were at Kenora. I wonder if you have time to help me find out something more about Nootsie Tah: Where was she from the time she was hurried away from Sacsahuaman and her mother until she came out of nowhere last summer to teach you about fairies?

I am asking your help now for I think—mind you I am not sure—that I have picked up her trail in England more than one hundred years ago. You may be able to follow it further, since the libraries in Toronto have so many more books than the Kingston libraries have.

Two men, John Keats and his friend Charles Brown, picked up part of the story. They say there were two princes who travelled long miles to find a "lost" princess (her real name, you and I know, is Nootsie Tah); they tell us of a dumb dwarf (you and I know very well that this is Grumpy, pretending to be dumb) and a green ape (whom I don't know at all); they tell of a lovely flower, like your blue pansy, that the princes were not to pick, if they were to see the princess.

One evening, just as the sun was setting, and their shadows stretched out ahead of them as if four giants were walking along, they saw this flower so blue, so fresh, so like the gem that the dwarf wore on his little finger, that they all stopped to look at it in wonderment. Then one of them—I do not know which one—reached down and picked it. "In a moment," so Keats and Brown say, "the flower drooped, withered, shrank almost to nothing, then into dust . . . Now the princess was lost! The princes stood like statues of grief: they could find no words to comfort one another."

*And while they were standing there, a fairy voice
called to them from almost overhead. Looking up they
saw, perched upon a slender bough, a bird of lovely form
and brilliant plumage." It sang this song to cheer them:*

> *Shed no tear—O, shed no tear!*
> *The flower will bloom another year.*
> *Weep no more! O! weep no more!*
> *Young buds sleep in the root's white core.*
> *Dry your eyes! O! dry your eyes,*
> *For I was taught in Paradise*
> *(For I was taught in Paradise)*
> *To ease my breast of melodies—*
>   *Shed no tear.*

> *Overhead! look overhead!*
> *'Mong the blossoms white and red—*
> *Look up, look up. I flutter now*
> *On this flush pomegranate bough.*
> *See me! 'tis this silvery bill*
> *Ever cures the good man's ill.*

Shed no tear! O shed no tear!
The flower will bloom another year.
Adieu, adieu—I fly, adieu,
I vanish in the heaven's blue—
  Adieu, adieu!

Keats called this story, I think, "The Fairies
Triumph." Here, in Kingston, I found only what I have
told you; in Toronto, you will probably find the whole
story. It is not likely that Keats knew that the bird singing
was Ariel.

Mention to your mother and father, the boys, and
Nancy that I wrote you and asked about them.

  Sincerely,
  R.C. Moir

The next summer we returned to the lake, happy and excited as always. And though there were no more letters from fairies, I had become a reader and the Kenora Public Library was my gateway into the enchanted world of books.

We had new neighbours at the lake—on the other side of our house from the Moirs—and they had grandchildren that I went to visit. They did everything differently there. They had a maid and they ate crustless sandwiches. They had a very big, very fast boat. And most wonderful of all, they had a little elevator on a railway track from the dock to the cottage. You sat on the chair and pressed a button and then the chair clattered up through the scrubby bushes to the top of the hill.

Mr. Moir and I continued to be friends, but as the summers went on and I grew older we spent less and less time together in the garden and the Ice House and beside the old pot-bellied stove in the book-lined inner room.

Nonetheless, Mr. Moir continued to write to me— usually at Christmas and always on my birthday in June.

When I was seven, Mr. Moir sent me some sticks he had carved and painted and polished. They were for doing complex math calculations, and were modelled on something used by the Phoenicians.

When I was about nine or ten, the Moirs decided that because of their age it was too difficult to keep up the cottage, and they sold it. We have a picture of them—the only one we have—on their last day at the lake, standing on their dock by their rowboat, dressed up to go into town.

We moved to England for a year. There was a gap in our correspondence.

The December after we returned I wrote to Mr. Moir. It had been some time since I had done so. I asked him if he remembered me.

Dear Miss Susan Coyne,

You ask in your card if we remember you. Mrs. Moir seems to remember you perfectly. I am getting old, and out of the fog that my memory has become a number of Susan Coynes emerge and disappear. Which one are you?

There was a Susan Coyne near some birch trees and an old outdoor fireplace, tethered so that she couldn't roll down into the lake. As I see her, she holds out her arms to be taken. Are you that Susan Coyne?

Then there was the Susan skipping along the paths in the garden, scolding me for tramping on the flowers. Are you that Susan Coyne?

And a Susan Coyne mended the dock with me, worked with sharp tools in the Ice House, worrying me so that I had to advise her father that he should count her fingers each time she went home. Are you she? She was delightful.

A Susan Coyne learning to swim. Learning to row a boat. A Susan Coyne looking for strawberries and currants, a Susan Coyne reading, a Susan Coyne saying, "If you don't see me tomorrow, Mr. Moir, you will know I've gone

visiting." Hardly any memories of Kenora without a
Susan Coyne somewhere. But which are you?

    Sincerely,
    R.C. Moir

P.S. Once I started a sermon on the power of Christian
names to deliver to one of those Susan Coynes. Some
tribes won't use a person's real name. They are afraid to.
In our country we have Miss Smith, Mr. Jones, Mrs.
Kowalchuk, and they are very careful in selecting the
people who may go behind those false fronts to meet
Isabelle, Harry or Rosita: some day I should like to tell
you about Susa, that city east of Babylon, of the river
Chasfes that flowed past it, of the Persian kings who
would drink water from no other river, and when they
went to war carried its water in silver jars mounted on a
train of four-wheel mule carts. I should like to tell you
how the first English Susan was named, and how she
came down from her tower high in the east to marry the
miller's son so that she could be near the millstream. The

*moral of it all is that no one named Susan should be tied
to a river or a lake. She may find that she can never
leave it, and will go to any extremity to stay near it.
Mind you, I don't think the miller's son was all that bad.*

All through junior high school, I wrote stories.
Sometimes I sent them to Mr. Moir. His responses
were unfailingly thoughtful and appreciative. He
ended one letter:

*And now, when I see a thin lean wasp, I suppose I
shall whisper to myself "Don't sneeze, he may be looking
for a fur coat."*

*How does it feel, Susan, when you put a few marks
on a white sheet of paper, to have a new kingdom and all
its people rise up in front of you?*

When I was fifteen I was among the first girls admitted to an all-boys school. My English teacher coached the hockey team. He told me my stories were "immature." I could see that this was true, and so I stopped writing stories altogether.

I got braces and covered my mouth when I smiled. My slump grew worse, which drove my mother crazy. She tried to put some steel in my spine. Every morning when I went off to catch the bus she would seize me by the shoulders and say, "Now remember, Susan: Attack!"

I did not tell much of this to Mr. Moir. But I did share with him my joy at discovering the world of theatre and play-acting. That June he sent me a birthday card:

I can't draw the birthday card I would send you, but I can tell you what to draw.

First you need a sheet of paper about this size. There is a high mountain on the right, and an impenetrable cloud on the left. They rise out of a level plain which takes up the rear of the sheet.

The mountain is going to be difficult. You must show it as rising out of the Sands of Time (for that is what the plain is) marking the end of fifteen years. There is no climbing it, no going back. However, it is not so high that one cannot see the light streaming over onto one figure at its foot.

Out of this mountain flow countless streams, some clear and sparkling, some murky, some even loathsome. These streams join to form a river, the river of time. You might find time to draw in people who find this river a source of pleasure or dread. (They tell me that the murky and loathsome streams tend to sink quickly into the sands.) Some people may seem to be too busy to pay much attention to the river; some will brood over it, the ones who say "leave me alone with my memories," and only their shadows join in the march across the plain.

All of that's immaterial detail. The chief figure is a girl (make her as lovely as you can), paying no attention to the mountain that has grown up behind her, eager only to get on with the journey that marks her sixteenth year towards the impenetrable clouds that mark the future. The light from the mountain top (having its origin eastward in Eden) shines on her. The poet describes it—

> She:
> "By the vision splendid
> Is on her way attended."

Can you show her hesitate just as she is about to take her first step while a look ("surprised by joy," a very great man has described it) comes over her face? What you are trying to show is her reaction to my well wishes, and the well wishes of all her friends. How she becomes aware of these wishes is your problem. Her joy is her response to us, and what a satisfying response it is.

A simple card, Susan, but it needs to be drawn just right.

Historical note: Mrs. Moir broke her hip in March and is making a satisfactory recovery.

My sincere wishes,
R.C.M.

Being a teenager, I suppose I did not take much note of the occasional references to failing health. Mr. Moir did not make much of them, preferring to tell me how he was learning to bake bread. And then in April of 1974 he wrote to thank me for my Easter letter, in which I had tried to put into words what I had felt about the Nootsie Tah letters.

Your unexpected Easter letter made us as happy as Coriolanus did Menenius. "It gives me an estate of seven years' health; in which time I will make a lip at the physician." Letters can have that effect.

*I am glad that Nootsie Tah remains one of the ties
that hold you to your part of Coney Island. That adds to
my enjoyment of it. I wonder if it would be too much to
ask you to take my place and admire a marsh marigold
that grows across the road from the end of the path that
starts at your place and crosses the Anderson lot. There
will be a path of a sort that takes you to Bay Point and
the Radcliffe's—the plant will be near this path and the
foot of the mountain. It will not be in bloom when you
see it in July, but it is the only one, and is almost a perfect specimen.*

> *Very specially,*
> *Yours sincerely,*
> *R.C.M.*

Mr. Moir died in early June. Soon after that, I
received a package in the mail from Mr. Moir's children. On the outside, written in Mr. Moir's handwrit-
ing, were the words, "Opened by mistake." I ripped
open the envelope and out fluttered a quantity of

crayoned drawings, several letters to Nootsie Tah, a small black and white photo of an artist's vision of the meeting between Titania and Oberon in *A Midsummer Night's Dream* and a miniature Pirate Hat, made of paper and decorated with a soft white feather.

> Shed no tear—O shed no tear!
> The flower will bloom another year.
> Weep no more! O! weep no more!
> Young buds sleep in the root's white core.

Ten years later, I graduated from theatre school and got my first job—playing Helena in an outdoor production of *A Midsummer Night's Dream*. (I studied history at university and briefly considered the idea of becoming a lawyer and joining the "R.W." It didn't take, alas—I think I realized that my "excessively emotional" nature might not be an asset at the bar.)

Every night, as the stars appeared in the sky above, I stood beside a flickering torch and listened to the song of the fairies as they lull Titania to sleep:

You spotted snakes with double tongue,
Thorny hedge hogs, be not seen;
Newts and blind-worms, do no wrong,
Come not near our fairy queen.

And every night I would see in my mind the magic fireplace, the moonlit slope, the pink paper folded in three and sealed with fairy wax, the winter road and the nodding pansies in Mr. Moir's beautiful garden.

It was my father who saved Nootsie Tah's letters for me.

My mother said if she'd known I was going to make a career out of being sensitive, she wouldn't have spent so much time trying to cure me of it.

I married the miller's son. We have a boy and a girl of our own now. And as they grow, I try to remember the love and respect for children and for the interconnectedness of all living things that I learned from my friend so long ago.

Three years ago, the children and I visited my parents in the cottage they now live in, in Keewatin, on the mainland. On the last day of our vacation my mother and the children and I took the boat and went over to the public beach on Coney Island for a picnic. Julia, who at three was rarely content, immediately threw herself down on the grass in tears of rage. I watched her in mute despair. "It will pass," my mother said, "It's such a short time that they're little." And then she suggested that I take my seven-year-old son for a walk along the winter road to see if we could find the path to the old cottage. So we set off along the track, while my mother stayed behind with Julia.

Along the way, Jamie said, "Tell me everything about when you were young," but I could not think of much to entertain him. I was tired and feeling slightly oppressed by a day spent trying to appease my cranky toddler.

When we finally found the path, it was so overgrown it was almost impossible to follow. I wondered whether my son really wanted to hack his way through the undergrowth, but he was determined. So we plunged in, breaking off branches and climbing over fallen trees. In truth, I could not tell if we were even heading in the right direction until we came upon a pile of timber that I recognized as the ruins of an old outhouse near the cottage. Beyond this was a clearing. My heart leapt unexpectedly as I spotted the familiar red roof.

Everything was just as I remembered it: the green and white cottage, the long silky grass, the mountain ash beside the dining room window, the huge yellow birch tree where I had been tethered as an infant.

Tiger lilies were in bloom beside the steps. We knocked on the door, but no one answered. Inside, the wicker furniture was still piled with my mother's chintz cushions and there was the braid rug in the middle room and even the glass wind chimes on the verandah. I had the eerie feeling that the others had just left to go for a ride in the boat. We stood for a moment, my little boy and I, listening to the wind in the trees and gazing out at the shimmering lake, at tiny Five Pines Island.

"Tell me more," my son urged, but I could not put into words all that I had felt about this place. "Let's take a look at Mr. Moir's house," I said, and I told him a little about the elderly gentleman who had lived next door: how I had helped him in his garden, and played chess with him, and how we had read books together beside the old stove. The little bungalow had been much altered and was now a modern-looking place suitable for a professional couple. Little of his remarkable garden remained. Standing there, I felt strangely ill at ease, and I told Jamie it was time to go.

But an impulse struck me and I called Jamie back. At the bottom of a long hedgerow, we got down on our hands and knees to peer beneath the leaves. It was dark, and we had to push the branches out of the way. A little bird, perched on one of the lower branches, eyed us suspiciously. And then we saw it—the old stone fireplace. It was smaller than I remembered it, about two feet wide, covered with lichen and moss, almost like an altar. "What is it?" my son asked. "It's a fireplace. And when I was a little younger than you . . ." I began, then stopped still, remembering. When I looked up Jamie's eyes were wide with expectation. "When I was a little younger than you I used to find letters here. Letters from a fairy." "Is that true?" he asked in a small voice, unsure of what he was hearing. "Yes," I said, "It's true." And I placed my hand on his silky hair to feel the heat from the sun. "It's a true story."

When we returned to the beach, I saw my tiny red-headed daughter Julia in the distance, waving to me. She and my mother had made a castle in the sand, and furnished it with shells and feathers and a moat filled with cool clear water.

Later that night, sitting on the dock and watching the moon spill her light across the dark lake, I thought of how many kinds of enchantments there are in this world. And I thought how right it was that Nootsie Tah got to go home to her mother, to Cuzco and Sacsahuaman, that high hill, to live in a New Temple of the Sun, where no doubt they are living still.

The Child's Toys & the Old Man's Reasons
Are Fruits of the Two Seasons.

Man was made for Joy & Woe;
And when this we rightly know,
Thro' the World we safely go,
Joy & Woe are woven fine,
A Clothing for the Soul divine;
Under every grief and pine
Runs a joy with silken twine.

William Blake

MR. MOIR'S QUOTATIONS

"I know a bank whereon the wild thyme blows . . ."
     Shakespeare, *A Midsummer Night's Dream*

"Before you can say, 'Come,' and 'Go' . . ."
     Shakespeare, *The Tempest*

"How beautiful must be . . ."
     Robert Bridges, "Nightingales"

"Not a mouse . . ."
     A Midsummer Night's Dream

"Where the bee sucks there suck I"
     The Tempest

"Her waggon-spokes are made of long spinners' legs . . ."
     Shakespeare, *Romeo and Juliet*

"Deck us all with Boston Charlie . . ."
     Walt Kelly, "The Pogo Christmas Carol"

"Malignant thing, dost thou forget . . ."
     The Tempest

"This is the Key of the Kingdom . . ."
     Traditional rhyme

"She is the fairies' midwife . . ."
        Romeo and Juliet

"Behold the chariot of the Faerie Queen . . ."
        Shelley, "Queen Mab"

"Wha's my Shepherd . . ."
        Traditional Scottish psalm

"Oh! Not the visioned poet in his dreams . . ."
        "Queen Mab"

"Siffle et sonne/ Tombe et tonne . . ."
        Algernon Charles Swinburne, *Chastelard*

"Le navire est à l'eau . . ."
        Chastelard

"Shed no tear—O, shed no tear . . ."
        John Keats, "Faery Bird's Song"

"By the vision splendid/ Is on her way attended . . ."
        Wordsworth, "Ode: Intimations of Immortality
        from Recollections of Early Childhood"

ACKNOWLEDGEMENTS

My mother has a saying, "A Ship is Safe in Harbour but that's Not what a Ship is For."

Many people have helped me pilot this little vessel out to sea. Chief amongst them is its first reader and greatest supporter, Albert Schultz, to whom I owe the greatest debt of thanks. I would also like to thank Robin Phillips, Urjo Kareda, Timothy Findley, Bill Whitehead, Jan Jaffe Kahn, Martha, Paula, Catherine, Nancy and Joe for their thoughtful comments on the manuscript.

Mr. Donald Moir, Mrs. Mary Tremblay and Mrs. Marie Moir all gave generously of their time and provided essential background material on their family. I thank them for their godspeed.

To Mr. Moir, who couldn't have known how he would affect my life: Thank you for the song. I liked it very much. With fondest love.

To my family: "As the twig is bent so grows the branch." This book is for them.

How does it feel, Susan, when you put a few marks on a white sheet of paper, to have a new kingdom and all its people rise up in front of you?

R. C. Moir